TIFFANY PRINCE

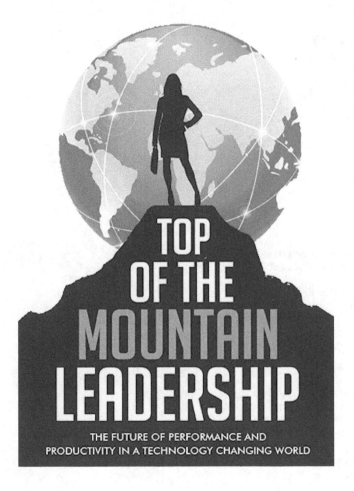

TOP
OF THE
MOUNTAIN
LEADERSHIP

THE FUTURE OF PERFORMANCE AND
PRODUCTIVITY IN A TECHNOLOGY CHANGING WORLD

Top of the Mountain Leadership
Copyright ©2019 Tiffany Prince

ISBN 978-1506-908-18-2 HC
ISBN 978-1506-908-19-9 PBK
ISBN 978-1506-908-20-5 EBK

LCCN 2019939482

April 2019

Published and Distributed by
First Edition Design Publishing, Inc.
P.O. Box 17646, Sarasota, FL 34276-3217
www.firsteditiondesignpublishing.com

To my husband, Karl, many thanks for all of the encouraging words and support.

To my family, for the encouragement to share my passion for great leadership.

Mike,

Thank you for sharing your wisdom with me. You inspired me. Good luck on your journey to the summit!

Tiffany

Table of Contents

Introduction

*"Remember this. Hold on to this. This is the
only perfection there is, the perfection of
helping others. This is the only thing we can
do that has any lasting value or meaning.
This is why we're here."*
Andre Agassi

I have a passion for leading and developing others. All around me, I've seen good and bad leaders. Among the good ones, I find it fascinating that it is so hard to describe what great leadership looks like. Even harder to describe is what you can do, in practical terms, to become a great leader. What I've found is that it takes a little bit of magic, some science, and a lot of self-determination.

My career has taken me to some amazing places around the world. Everywhere I've been, what I've noticed—no matter the culture of an organization—is that there are fundamentals to leading teams for greater purpose. The methods in how we do it may vary, but the "what" remains the same. Leading humans toward a goal is like flying multiple kites on a windy day. As you lead, there is always something else you can work to perfect. There are logical and emotional aspects to every relationship that need to be considered, and every one of us has a different mix of preferences. This can make leading others feel daunting at times, even mentally draining. But I promise you, it is worth the effort when you start to see your employees fulfill their full potential.

In my life, I have held multiple leadership roles. I just gravitate to them or they choose me; I am not sure which happens first. My first memorable leadership role was when I became the captain of the junior varsity cheerleading team. It was only my second year as a cheerleader, and I decided to put myself in the running for captain. So, it surprised some of the more seasoned cheerleaders that people on the squad voted for me. To be honest, I was also surprised. But I put myself out there, so I needed to figure it out. I wouldn't say I was the best at being the leader at that time. I ran into politics within the squad, some resentment, and even outright disregard for me, but I took it in stride. I truly believed some members of the squad just didn't see my potential as a leader.

My point in bringing this example up is that you will not please everyone as a leader. Your preferred leadership style may not be in sync with everyone's needs or desires in a leader. That is okay, which is what I had to learn. What I didn't understand at the time was that you need to flex your leadership style sometimes for key individuals. If you have top talent on your team, it is *your* responsibility to figure out how to motivate them. I am sure you have seen leaders who present themselves the same way all the time regardless of the situation. In some circumstances that is fine, but in these competitive times, more is required of our leaders.

A Lifelong Journey

"There is no elevator to success. You have to take the stairs."
Zig Ziglar

I've come a long way from those times in high school but have continued to be fascinated by the nuances of leadership. I am an eternal student and observer of leadership in all forms. In my experience, research, and interviews, I have found some amazing ways to practically demonstrate skills that will put you ahead of everyone else. To be successful, you need to endure situations that may not be that comfortable for you, and you also have to have some humility. As you gain experience, you will also gain confidence, which will feed into being a great leader. As I remind you throughout this book, leadership is a lifelong journey.

An Uncertain Future

There is a lot of buzz out there around technology and the speed of change. Every year artificial intelligence (AI) capabilities are getting better. In some tasks, AI can outperform a human. What does this mean for the future of work, and how do we prepare our teams for this future? In the research I have conducted, I have found ways to get teams ahead of the massive changes that are coming. I also have collected insights from more than 20 leaders of various organizations and industries around the globe—leaders on the foreground of these changes.

The initial response I get from those with whom I have spoken about artificial intelligence is fear of the unknown. I will go into more detail about what I discovered to be the evolving truths and what we might anticipate. In addition, I uncovered the key skill sets that will be needed in the near future. I will walk through those attributes in more detail too. My honest opinion is that if we start to prepare our workforce now and are proactive, then we have nothing to fear. But we will also need to have an open mind and be flexible, because there is a lot we still don't know. We will need to figure it out together.

Our organizational structures and teaming will most certainly change from how things generally function today. Agility within organizations will be key to being competitive. Decisions will be made closer to where the actual work is being done, and leadership will look and feel differently. Our workforces will be smarter, faster, and evolve more quickly than ever before.

The key to all of these changes is the amount and quality of data we will have and will gather throughout the coming years. Data is king, and how we use it will determine whether we are successful or not. As a Harvard business professor suggested to me, dust off your old statistics and linear algebra books. I guess our high school teachers were right about algebra; the need for it just came 30–50 years later than expected for most of us. Don't worry if you didn't keep those books. You can find free courses online at sites such as the Khan Academy that can help anyone brush up on his or her knowledge.

What's in This Book

This book is about Top of the Mountain Leadership. Based on my research, I found it is hard to define what great leadership looks like, so I constructed a scaffolding as a way for others to visualize quality leadership and the impact it can have. I welcome your thoughts on it as well as I am sure it will evolve over time.

In *Top of the Mountain Leadership,* leaders will explore how to:
- Engage and motivate employees
- Help employees reach their true potential
- Secure the best talent for your team
- Build truly diverse and inclusive teams
- Navigate global and virtual teams in practical ways
- Develop a true and human connection with employees

Leadership Growth Plan

As you navigate through these changes, it will take dedicated time and effort. To be more successful in completing your goals, think about what you want to accomplish and why it is important to you. Take a few minutes right now and assess why you chose *Top of the Mountain Leadership.* Think about how you will apply the principles of leadership described here and what areas you would like to focus on in your journey.

1. Some areas of growth in my leadership that I would like to explore:

2. Some challenges I might face in testing new skills and knowledge:

3. Amount of time I am willing to commit each week to developing these skills:

4. I have identified an accountability partner (someone who can give me feedback and hold me to my commitment to grow as a leader). That person is:

Good luck on your journey to the summit!

Bringing Out the Very Best in Your Teams

I will never forget the first team I led as a professional. Leadership is a daunting responsibility and, like most of us, I was thrown into the role without any formal leadership training or coaching. To be honest, I didn't understand the difference between being an individual contributor and a leader of a team. I realized quickly that if I wanted to be successful, I needed to research great leadership myself. This is where I started my journey toward being a leader that my team would follow anywhere. That was my aspiration. Your aspiration may be different, but I can assure you that the road to becoming a great leader is much more fulfilling than simply acting as a manager who is focused only on tasks and projects.

We are at a moment in time where views of leadership and the expectations from our teams are changing. Old ways of command and control leadership styles from the Industrial Age are not appropriate for the work of the future. Developing and encouraging our teams on an individual basis are becoming the new expectations of leaders. Just as technology is becoming ever more personalized, so must our leadership and coaching of others. In this chapter, we will explore various leadership styles and how they potentially impact the effectiveness of your teams.

As leaders, we want to ensure that our teams are performing smoothly and efficiently toward accomplishing the organization's goals. Many of us have experienced varying leadership styles during our careers and know how important they are in developing our teams. In fact, style can make the difference between success and failure. Research from the Center for Creative Leadership[1] has shown that 38% of executives fail in the first 18 months. Failed leadership is a crisis of our times, and there are many gaps to fill. How will your natural leadership style impact your team, and does your style match what your team needs? Do you ask yourself, how can I be a better leader? Exploring these questions may reveal why teams of people follow some leaders and not others.

Topics covered in this chapter include:

- Five leadership styles
- Ways to leverage leadership styles
- Attributes of great leadership
- Characteristics of failed leadership

Five Leadership Styles

In my research, experience, and observations, I have discovered five key leadership styles that lead to higher-performing teams and greater business impact. You will see the leadership styles are tied to famous mountains. I believe that the journey to great leadership is like planning to hike any great mountain. It takes time, planning and dedication in order to have a successful trip. Think of your career in a leadership position like climbing a mountain. You need to take steps every day to be a better leader. Some days will be better than others and you will have challenges along the way. However, if you persevere through these bumps in the journey you will eventually reach the summit. To have the most influence on the performance of your team and organization, you need to understand and flex all five styles of leadership outlined here. You may find yourself gravitating to one or two of the leadership styles more than the others. That is normal and expected. But to be a great leader, you need to understand and situationally leverage all five styles. Let's go into detail on each of the five styles now.

Everest

The Everest style describes leaders who are results-oriented, focused on outcomes. They are drivers in the organization and like assuming authority. They are quick to accept challenges, but also expect to be rewarded well for obtaining targets and goals. They don't mind taking risks, as necessary, especially if doing so could give them an advantage. These leaders are competitive and strive for excellence in themselves and others.

I recently worked with a leader who embodied this style completely. Because she had been so successful in driving other projects, especially those that seemed unobtainable, she was given the opportunity to take over an initiative that was stuck in the same spot for a few years. She accepted this role as a welcome challenge. She assumed authority and was used to pushing herself and others to achieve high standards. When the team didn't get behind her drive for results, she couldn't understand what was wrong. She became very frustrated with the team members. I took this opportunity to coach this individual on leveraging other leadership styles. I believe that where she stumbled was jumping in before developing relationships with the other team members. They saw her as a pushy "my-way-or-the-highway" person, which didn't sit well with them. When she got stuck and couldn't make progress in this initiative, I asked her to put herself in her team members' shoes and see whether she could come up with some incentives for them to complete the project. By showing how valuable the team was to this initiative and to the company in general, she encouraged the team members to push through and complete the tasks before the end of the year. They also won a company-wide award in recognition of their efforts.

Where I have seen the Everest leadership style work well is when the organization has a well-understood vision and strategy. These leaders can drive the results and will direct even team members who are not in line with their thinking to follow where they are driving. Employees that thrive under this style are motivated to obtain results as well and are open to having this type of leader be more directive when necessary if the leader sees it as a better way to obtain those results.

There is usually not a lot of coaching or developing of people or teams with this style. These leaders are focused on the organizational goals and are not concerned with developing their team members. They may not even understand their team's strengths or be able to leverage the collective experience of the team. They have a clear vision of how things should be done and want to see that carried through without challenges. They don't have time to get people to understand the vision because they are so focused on the outcome and achievement of the goal as the most important factor.

I think a good example of this type of leadership is Jeff Bezos, the CEO of Amazon®. He is extremely results-oriented and has a hyper focus on his customer. This style is very intense and can burn out employees if applied as the sole leadership style, especially if the rest of the team is not receptive to that style. As with all leadership styles, each one has its own strengths and challenges.

Denali

The second leadership style is Denali. These leaders are relationship-oriented. They are very good at coaching and mentoring others. They want to ensure that employees reach their potential and are valued within the organization. Their style aligns well with what is called the *servant leader,* which is characterized by the approach of removing obstacles and providing team members what they need to get their jobs done. In this way, they are committed to the growth of their employees and teams. They are also known for being good listeners.

This leadership style works well when the team is committed and they are motivated to achieve goals. These leaders understand where each employee is in his or her development and what motivates these individuals to achieve. They will not tell others how to do their jobs; that is up to them. These leaders are more focused on establishing and maintaining the right environment for the team to do great things. Most employees want to work for this type of leader.

Another leader I worked with who had this particular style as his dominant leadership style was respected and loved by his team. However, in this situation, the company was going through some hard times and needed to change things up if the company was to survive in the future. Because this leader valued the relationships on the team more than driving for results and making changes, he was being pressured to leave the company. He didn't understand why there was an issue, because his team was very happy. In this instance, I coached him on the balance between keeping a positive relationship with his team and driving for results. The change was difficult, at first, because it did not feel comfortable to this leader. I asked him to start with small requests to the team and to paint the picture of why it was important for the team to drive in that direction. Over the course of a few months, he became much more comfortable with applying some pressure on the team to push boundaries and take some risks. The new approach ended up paying off; the team created a new product, and it became the number one seller of the company. The sales team loved it because it was exactly what customers were asking for, and the competition didn't have a product like this in the market yet. This team is now working on the company's next blockbuster product.

This style can be challenging for some teams and employees if the organization doesn't have a clear vision or goals. These leaders are not directive and will let the team decide the best way forward. When teammates disagree or have diverse thoughts on how to do things, it can be challenging for these leaders, who are focused more on the individual development level. They thrive when there is harmony on the team. Dealing with conflict can be difficult in this leadership style because these leaders don't want to hurt anyone's feelings.

An example of someone who embodies the Denali style was Mother Teresa. She met others where they were and transformed them to care for others as well. She leveraged her relationships with others to touch others' lives. She understood people from all walks of life, and her power of influence was the key to her success. This stance serves leaders well in organizations as well as in other aspects of life. It can be very powerful and, unfortunately, in this day and age, underutilized. Getting to know your team's strengths and needs can allow you to coach and develop them into better employees and leaders themselves. Most employees embrace this style of leadership.

Mount Fuji

The Mount Fuji leaders are visionary in their leadership style. As you might imagine, they are dynamic and entrepreneurial while paving new paths. In looking to the future, they push the boundaries in what can be done; instead of asking "why?" they ask, "why not?" I see many startup business owners having this mindset because they are generally innovators. They want to transform businesses and provide support in tackling obstacles to success while creating new products or services.

These are the leaders who can successfully set the tone and direction of any business. People will follow these leaders because they have influence and can be charismatic. Employees need to understand the purpose of their work so they can understand the business's direction and impact. These leaders can paint a clear picture so everyone knows the "what" and "why" of their business.

Alternatively, this leadership style can be detrimental if the vision is ever-evolving and nothing seems to get accomplished. If the target keeps moving without small successes or at least testing and trying new things, employees can get frustrated by the lack of results or direction. As with all styles, these leaders need to find a balance between guiding others and allowing team members to deliver results while keeping a look out to the future of their business.

I have found that a lot of smaller business owners have this type of leadership style. It makes sense because you have to be passionate and have a vision to create a new company, product, or service. I have seen this leadership style thrive in the beginning stages of companies because it drives the energy and enthusiasm of the team. Once companies hit a certain threshold, however, this style becomes less effective if leaders haven't built a team around them that complements their primarily visionary style. I saw this with a client I worked with recently. His business was growing and he was opening new locations. From the outside, the business seemed very successful. Where I came in was helping to develop some foundational operations to help the company successfully continue its growth. I saw an opportunity to work with this leader on his leadership style. He clearly had a vision of where he wanted to take his business—from a regional to a national level. I appreciated the ambition of this leader. Yet, as he was pushing the organization to reach this vision, he didn't spend time addressing some foundational issues such as employee turnover rate and building systems to support a high volume of projects. I worked with him to recruit someone for a new position responsible for operations of the company—to address these issues and to dive into the details of what it would take to build a foundation. After a few months on board, this new leader lifted the burden of the day-to-day operations off of the business owner. He could then focus on the longer-term vision of driving toward a national presence with his business, and the new leader helped to create a sustainable model that would grow with the company.

A good example of a famous visionary leader was Steve Jobs, the former CEO of Apple®. His focus on the future in driving new and innovative products shifted the marketplace forever, starting with the iPod® and continuing today with the iPad® and iPhone®. He also created such a strong chemistry with his customers that they are very brand loyal, which is hard to accomplish and maintain in the market today.

Mont Blanc

In looking at the next leadership style, Mont Blanc, these are what I call the reflective leaders. These leaders like to think things through before they act. They are not comfortable going on gut reactions and want assurance that things have been properly thought out. As you can imagine, they are very analytical and maintain order and logic under their control. If there is a process, they will follow it and are comfortable with the order it provides.

I see many of these leaders as computer scientist, accountants, scientists, and engineers. The nature of their work lends itself to this style. They tend to be detail-oriented and can make sense of large amounts of data, which is a great skill to have in today's age. Employees can learn a lot from them about how to gather and manage data. Mont Blanc leaders have mastered the art of making sense of copious amounts of it in their roles. Strong leaders take the time to step back and reflect on what they have learned, which is so important in this complex and ever-changing world we now live in.

I recently worked with a client who demonstrated this type of leadership style. She was wondering why she wasn't getting promoted, so she hired me to coach her. As she walked me through her situation, I noticed that she was most definitely strong in a reflective style of leadership. I thought it would be good to also interview her team to gain some insights into their concerns in working with her. While the team appreciated the structure this leader provided, they were wishing she would be more personal. The relationship seemed very robotic, and they were frustrated that they couldn't really take risks or be innovative. This insight was extremely valuable, so when sitting down with this leader, I asked how she felt about building relationships and letting go more. Her answer surprised me, but now that I reflect back on it, I can see why she came to this conclusion.

She was worried about getting too close to any employees and felt she couldn't have difficult conversations in the future if she had a personal relationship with them. What she didn't realize is that not having a relationship was having an opposite effect. The team members heard from her only if they did something wrong and never received praise. I asked her to find ways to incorporate some recognition into her weekly communications with the team. She resisted at first, but then she saw the power this little gesture had on her team members and their willingness to do a good job. She told me that all the tension and frustrations from the team started to melt away. She didn't feel as if she was all alone anymore, and the team really connected at a different level with her. She learned things about her team she didn't know. When I later spoke with the team members about the changes, they were very enthusiastic and encouraged that they were given projects that they felt may not have been delegated earlier. It wasn't long before this leader ended up getting promoted within the company.

This leadership style can be discouraging for some employees, especially if they are not oriented the same way. The employees may have trouble communicating with this type of leader. I have seen projects rejected because employees were not ready to dive into the details of their proposals with this type of leader.

Richard Branson, CEO of the Virgin Group, is known as a reflective leader. He routinely steps away from his business to digest new information and to think about trends in the market. He is a master at broadening his perspective by trying new things and thinking about what can translate back into his broad range of businesses.

Matterhorn

The final leadership style I am introducing is the inclusive leader, Matterhorn. These leaders seek collaboration and diversity on their teams in order to obtain the best ideas. I have seen many of these leaders demonstrate a strong sense of cultural intelligence, because they are open-minded and willing to adapt along with considering the multiple viewpoints of others.

These leaders thrive in cross-functional and matrix teams within organizations. They are savvy at building a large network of colleagues with whom they can communicate and explore options. Many teams appreciate this leadership style because these leaders break down barriers and open up communication within the team.

Employees who like to make decisions quickly or are results-oriented can have challenges with this leadership style. In seeking to drive collaboration, decisions or actions can take longer. However, that being said, once a decision is made, these leaders tend to produce more successful or productive outcomes or results. It is one of those cases in which you need to slow down to speed up. In cultures that are more focused on individual results and not team oriented, this type of leadership can be annoying at times.

Nelson Mandela was a great example of an inclusive leader. He overcame many obstacles in his rise to the Presidency of South Africa after apartheid ended. His leadership style was to bring all the parties together, even those who imprisoned him, in order to move the country forward. He partnered with his disparate colleagues to pave a new path for the country. I would imagine this would be difficult for anyone in his situation to do, but he understood this style would produce the most positive outcomes for all.

Ways to Leverage Leadership Styles

The successful practice of the traits of these leadership styles is tied to how well a leader communicates in particular circumstances. We all have our default style that we are comfortable in using. It may stem from how we were raised and what styles we saw growing up, or it may be driven by our personality types. Having a default style is fine and a good starting point. We need to know which of those styles we default to and why. But here is the key to shifting from good to great: A great leader is able to leverage other leadership styles that are needed in a given situation, but are not that leader's predominant style. It is those leaders who can, in the moment, provide what is needed for the team and not just for themselves. This is the key to success. It is not about you, but the team! If you can get this right, you will have people who will follow you wherever you go. Have you seen leaders who fit this category? Did you see them shift their style to meet the team's needs?

From my observations and my experience as a leader and in helping other leaders become better leaders, I have identified some common leadership traits. In leveraging these traits and behaviors well, some leaders can stand out from other leaders. These traits and behaviors are based in these essential elements:

- Communication style
- Conflict style/preference
- Recognition of other's achievements
- Coaching/feedback
- Self-awareness
- Dealing with ambiguity
- Change leadership

Each of these items is measured in degrees, on a scale or continuum. How we handle ourselves as leaders in the moment day after day is how we are measured by our teams. Some key behaviors, when practiced consistently, can have a huge impact on a team's effectiveness.

Regardless of your predominant leadership style, following are some essential steps for successful leadership:

- Understand each of your team member's preferred leadership style.
- Deliver customized/personalized leadership to each team member.
- Recognize nonverbal cues in reaction to your words and actions; adjust as needed.
- Avoid derailing behaviors (remember, you are the positive influence and representative of the organization and of what it is trying to accomplish).
- Most of all, be authentic! People appreciate real leaders.

I will give you an example from my personal experience. I was leading a team for a government contract. My default style is very trusting and collaborative with my team. You could say I am a mix of the Everest and Matterhorn leadership styles: I define what I expect of my team members and they deliver. I would also describe myself as results-driven. Do what you say you are going to do in the time you say you will do it. For those teammates that are experienced, this style works well because they do not want to be micromanaged. What I didn't realize is that a few employees on my team were more comfortable or performed better when they were given very directive instructions.

In this situation, we were working on multiple work streams, and each team member was expected to meet his or her deadlines. I thought that if I identified what they needed to do that I did not need to tell them how to do it. On this particular week, we had some huge deliverables. At the beginning of the week, I gave the direction of what we needed to deliver to the client that week. Like most leaders, I had more tasks and deadlines to focus on than hours in the week, so I just assumed everyone was clear and working on what was needed to meet this end-of-week goal for our client. Reality was very different! When we got to the end of the week, half the deliverables were not finished, which took me and my client by surprise. We all looked bad because we did not give the client what was needed at the time we had promised. This was a big lesson for me, and I vowed not to repeat that situation again.

I took a hard look at what went wrong. How did we get to this point? Why didn't the team members deliver what they said they would? I started looking into the situation with an inquisitive stance versus being accusatory. I was trying to find out what I could do better the next time to support my team. What I found out is that I was not available to answer some critical questions about the work to be done. The team was stuck and didn't have a lifeline to get out of the hole they were in, which meant they could not move forward. Because I didn't take time to check in and make sure adequate progress was being made and to answer any questions, the team members felt they did not have the support needed to be successful. They were afraid to say anything because I did not seem open to providing feedback or making the time for them. Big mistake!

That situation changed the way I managed teams moving forward. I am more willing to adjust my style of leadership to meet the needs of the team, not the other way around. To adjust my style, I need to understand which style will work best in a particular situation. As I mentioned earlier, I am a mix of Everest and Matterhorn leadership styles. I have to flex my leadership muscle especially when I need to apply the Mont Blanc leadership style. This takes a bit of practice but is worth the effort. I realized that in some instances my team will require more structure and guidance. I may need to sit with them and walk them through how something is done. Doing this allows the team to understand my thought process and to gain some insights along the way. I also get to see how the team members approach a problem or situation so I can start to get a feel for their leadership preference. In adjusting my style, I am able to produce better business results, and that is what we all want at the end of the day.

What are some typical leadership styles you can leverage? Don't worry if you are less skillful in certain areas. These skills are something that can be practiced and refined over time. It may take a few tries before you get it right, but believe me, your team will notice and appreciate the effort.

Nine Attributes of Great Leadership

In my interviews with various leaders across industries and positions, I was curious to know what these individuals defined as a great leader. Surprisingly, this is a difficult question to answer. There seems to be no definitive way to describe great leadership, but we all agreed you know it when you see it or experience it. That being said, there are some commonalities of soft skills that seem to run through the descriptions given to me, which I will summarize here.

1. **Self-awareness.** By far, the number one skill brought up was having a clear understanding of yourself, including your strengths and weaknesses. This skill seems to be the foundational trait of great leaders around the world. It is also one of the tenants of emotional intelligence.

2. **Fairness in dealing with others**. Your team is watching how you handle situations and is judging you on your actions. Don't get me wrong; dealing fairly does not mean you have to give everyone exactly the same opportunities. Fairness is more about meeting others where they are and being fair in a given situation. Being respectful and trustworthy are keys to building this attribute. This attribute is tied to your unconscious biases. We all have biases but discerning in what blind spots or areas you have them can help you recognize them when they appear. By becoming aware of these, you can try to mitigate or explore the reasons for having these biases.

3. **Steadfastness**. You might wonder why I include this as an attribute but know that it will be key in helping your team navigate the expedited changes that are expected. We want leaders who in times of turmoil seem to hold steady and help the team through the challenge. If a leader responds emotionally to every perceived threat, then the team will not feel safe and, therefore, will sense a lack of leadership. Team members are looking for leaders to make decisions and provide direction, when appropriate, especially in times of change.

4. **Understanding of one's contribution to the business**. At the end of the day, we need to have happy customers regardless of the industry we work in. Being able to tie customer satisfaction with delivery of business results, and knowing exactly how your team contributes are keys to success. The ability to articulate the value of the work in the context of the team goals is a differentiator of a great leader.

5. **Willingness to go beyond one's job description**. Those of us who have been leaders within organizations or even within our communities and families know it takes hard work to become a leader that others will follow. Our job descriptions rarely define what we actually do and, as jobs flex and mold

to the new technologies being implemented, we will need to flex with them. This quality also means jumping in when needed. Showing a willingness to roll up your sleeves in order for the team to meet the goal goes a long way in demonstrating the values you expect of the team.

6. **Harmonious**. Great leaders need to work well with others. Building a network not only within your current company, but beyond, will serve you well as a leader. Your network gives you a knowledge pool to tap into when a situation is not quite clear. Think about a team that wasn't high performing. I guarantee that leader was not well-respected or networked. We need connections to make teams work.

7. **Empathetic**. This attribute is tied closely with self-awareness but is about the team's needs versus your strengths and weaknesses. Knowing how teams work and what motivates individuals will help drive teams to perform at a higher level. You need to listen to your team members' problems to help guide them to solve the challenges they are having. As we are paving a new way of working, we will come across many challenges that we just don't have answers for. In working together and letting your team know you share their pain points, it will help build trust and respect.

8. **Responsible**. To be an effective leader, you must develop others. It is your number one responsibility. This may mean taking some risks, which will mean your team will make some mistakes. Think of the mistakes as learning opportunities and allow space for your employees to gain new skills with guidance. I also believe in sheltering your team from some of the political sides of any organization. This may mean taking one for the team, but doing so allows the team to focus on the task at hand and not on other organizational worries.

9. **Confidence**. You need to hold fast in your ability to lead a team. You will have others challenge you and your authority at times. However, if you are solid in your belief of your knowledge and experience to lead teams, you will build the trust and respect that will convert your team to followers. I am not saying you have all the answers all the time or that you bulldoze over anyone's opinions. Confidence is more of an internal feeling that you can do this; being confident will provide the rudder needed to help the team navigate the murky waters of the unknown.

All of these attributes contribute to being a great leader. You may look at this list and realize you have some work to do in some of these areas. That is okay and is expected. The best leaders understand where their weaknesses are and are constantly honing their skills. The point is to identify which areas you are naturally attuned to and build from there. The more of these attributes you can strive for, the better off you will be.

Characteristics of Failed Leadership

Now, we all have had the opposite of a great leader in our careers. I think it is important to point out unwanted traits so that we don't fall into the trap of others before us. Many of the items listed here are important to be aware of as you transition from an individual contributor to a first-line manager but I also see these characteristics in seasoned leaders as well. The expectations are different when you are leading others, and what you do will change as well. Let's explore some pitfalls seen in leaders.

- **Taking on too much.** I see this time and time again. You have to understand that delegation is your friend and the only way you will be an effective leader. My perfectionists out there will have a hard time with this one (believe me, I struggled with this as well). When you take a role as a leader, you will actually need to juggle more things than in your previous role. It is not just about you and your performance anymore; you are being judged by the performance of your team. If you try to dictate how all the tasks are done or try to do most of it yourself just because it is easier and faster, that is the quickest way to drown yourself in frustration and defeat.

- **Setting up others to fail.** Your team will know exactly when this is happening. Mostly I have seen this in the form of unrealistic goals. Saying yes to everything and all requests does not serve you or your team well. I understand you cannot say no all the time either. You have to find the balance and become a good negotiator of what you think your team can accomplish in any given time frame. Burnout is a real thing and will cost you dearly in lost productivity.

- **Fear of competition from others.** This can come from within your team or from other parts of the organization. The best leaders are always thinking about their replacement and succession planning. Do not see the employees on your team as a threat. In fact, the best leaders see building out future leaders as a sign of accomplishment. Think about this for a moment. In helping others in their development, you are giving them meaningful skills that help the organization overall. If they choose to move to other parts of the organization, that only enhances your network and builds connections in new areas. Also, if you are not grooming your replacement, then who will take over for you when a new role opens that interests you? We rarely stay in jobs for more than 2 or 3 years now. So, why not build the best team you can in that time?

- **Stuck in what used to work.** This one is particularly dangerous for the future of our organizations. If you wait or procrastinate to act on new ideas or ways of work, your company will be in serious danger of failure, and quickly. Innovation and creativity will be vital to the survival of organizations in this tech-driven world of the future. We need to get savvy in solving problems and testing new approaches, even if they seem similar to something we have tried before. We are in a new environment, so why not try?

- **Putting your ego before the team.** I am sure many of you have experienced leaders who took the credit for any success of the team. By not recognizing others, you are reducing their loyalty and sending the message that you will not look out for the best interest of the team. When things don't go very well, do you throw others "under the bus"? How did that feel when others did that to you? When you are a leader, it is imperative to reward and recognize both individual and team efforts. If you don't, I assure you that your turnover on the team will be high. Your team members will go work for a leader who shows respect to all and doesn't just look out for his or her own best interest.

- **Using title as power.** Just because you have a leadership title (e.g., manager, director, executive, CEO) does not mean your employees have to respect or follow you. You need to earn that respect. Yes, you have worked hard to obtain this leadership role but with every rung you climb you have to build trust and respect all over again. Instilling fear by your leadership authority is not the way to win the hearts and minds of your employees.

- **Lack of a strong network.** If you think in this day and age you can know everything there is to know, you are setting yourself up for failure. Gone are the days that you stay with one or two job tracks within a company. In my research[2] I found that most employees will have four or five new careers (not just jobs, but wholesale changes in job descriptions) in the next 10 to 15 years. Your network will dictate how well you will navigate this new landscape. You need to foster and build out your network constantly because you never know when you may need to call in a favor.

As you can see, leadership is indeed difficult to define. There are many elements when it comes to being a great leader. No one trait is better than the others. It is the combination of these attributes and skills put into practice on a regular basis that creates great leaders.

Leadership is a journey, not a destination.

Key Takeaways:

- ✓ Just as technology has become more personalized, so must leadership.

- ✓ There are five key leadership styles that are needed in the future. Leaders need to flex all five styles and know when to do so to be effective and influential.

- ✓ These five leadership styles encompass outcomes, relationships, vision, reflection, and inclusion.

- ✓ Leaders can take steps to demonstrate the right traits and behaviors to motivate, influence, and engage their teams.

- ✓ Those who are seen as great leaders within organizations embody nine leadership attributes, apply them consistently, and have high-performing teams.

- ✓ Recognizing behaviors that might be derailing is a trait of a great leader. Leaders must put a plan together to undo these behaviors, which detract from great leadership.

Aligning Your Organization's Talent Needs

Finding and keeping good talent is a challenge for most organizations. Add to that how fast things are changing in this complex and volatile world, and it is hard for companies to keep up. While senior leadership is building and planning strategies, we need to think about the talent pool within and outside our organization to determine how to best plan for and align employees for the work of the future.

We spend lots of time in strategic planning mode beginning with identifying the right goals, setting budgets, and considering new innovations. As leaders, we may be involved in these conversations. As decisions are made, they get handed off and distributed throughout the organization. Unfortunately, communications can get watered down and seem disconnected.

In addition, executives can lose sight of what is happening at the ground level. Unfortunately, plans are a rearview mirror as the information we have reflects the past. This is why we need to do our best to foresee the future and plan accordingly throughout all levels of the organization.

From a talent perspective, I will outline ways to tackle this across the organization holistically in this chapter.

Topics covered in this chapter include:

- Communicating strategy
- Aligning strategy and workforce
- 3 Pillars Model
- Succession planning
- Skills-gap analysis
- Performance needs

Communicating Strategy

It is important for employees across the organization, at all levels, to internalize a strategy. They need to understand how their role is contributing to the strategic goals. Knowing the organization's goals will help employees chose the right tasks to prioritize and execute to move initiatives forward for the company. At the various leadership levels, balancing strategy and execution can be challenging. A recent *Harvard Business Review* study found that very few top leaders are good at both developing company strategies and executing against those strategies.[3] Only 23% of those leaders surveyed felt effective at doing both. This disconnect is a challenge for organizations because the balance of strategic planning with executing against it effectively will be the differentiator for successful companies of the future.

Communicating the strategy to others in a meaningful way is also a complicated imperative. I find that companies develop communication plans that are mostly based on one-way communication and pushed out to employees. This is not the most effective way to drive change or push for new horizons. The communication needs to be two-way and constant for employees to understand how the strategic plan relates to them. Think of your communication plan as an engagement strategy. It is not the quantity of communications sent to employees, but rather the quality of the messages that matter and what will have an impact long-term. A critical skill for more impactful leaders is top-notch communication skills.

Aligning Strategy and Workforce

When it comes to talent strategies, most organizations just don't get it. Organizations have high expectations for their employees. They expect them to already have the needed skills or they set out to hire those with the right skill sets. This approach has become a poor strategy for organizations. Millions of jobs need to be filled, but organizations can't seem to find the right fit or the right skill sets in one person. To add to the problem, organizations have not been investing in employee and professional development for the last 10–15 years, leaving the responsibility for any development to the employee. We are facing a talent war that is only going to get worse as we search for the ever-elusive "unicorn" employee. Ready, Hill and Thomas[4] argued in their *Harvard Business Review* article "Building a Game-Changing Talent Strategy" that leaders who are skeptical about making substantial and continual investments in their people have already lost the war for talent. This reality is made worse by the current low rate of unemployment and the number of job openings outnumbering those who are looking for work.

Because few employees have upskilled themselves and there was a lack of investment in employee's development, it has left organizations with a severe shortage of highly skilled employees with the right stuff. To address this gap, both employees and organizations need strategies for developing people that align with the organizational strategies. By creating a roadmap for success in partnership with key departments, you are better able to drive results throughout the organization and understand its capabilities. A recent study of 700 CEOs globally revealed that human capital management is their top priority[5]. Unfortunately, most organizations are doing no workforce planning of any kind. How do we know which are the most critical roles and skills that will drive results and ultimately the desired outcomes? Do we understand where the current gaps in skills are among employees? To answer these questions and develop a people strategy, I recommend partnering with both your Human Resources (HR) Department (or Human Resource Business Partners) and your Talent Management/Learning Department to pull together a plan of action. These departments can help build out a plan to address these gaps in skills, knowledge, and abilities for you and your organization. You first need to garner support from several areas of the company or organization to make this goal become reality.

I have worked with companies to align strategic direction with workforce needs. For example, there was a large high-tech firm headquartered in Germany that sent out a 30-page RFP (Request for Proposal) for a consultant to implement company-wide professional development. The RFP was extremely detailed, down to the specific learning objectives, and, of course, restricted to a certain number of days for training. The expectation was for the consultant to cover all the stated objectives regardless of the limited time. There was quite a laundry list of skills, many of which were open to interpretation, such as "develop presentation skills." In response to the RFP, I had to propose specifically how we would do this, without the benefit of talking to the actual employees who would be impacted. This was probably the most difficult project I had tackled in my career up to that point. The reason it was so hard is because the Human Resources representative in charge of this initiative was handed a legacy curriculum, and the leadership wanted to replicate that program. Further complicating the project was that two companies and cultures were being merged, and no real conversation was had around how these disparate workforces were trained previously or how big the gaps were in their knowledge of these subjects.

To overcome this challenge, I asked to interview various stakeholders that were tied to this initiative to better understand how best to support this training program and make it successful. When I dove a bit deeper with senior managers and new project leads, I started to understand that the target employees fell into two camps. One group already had some training, and the leadership was looking to build on those foundational skill sets to take them to the next level. The other group was completely new to these skills. If we built the training one-size-fits-all, as we were asked to do, it would not have the impact that the business desired. Additionally, we would have frustrated employees with training that would be too basic or too advanced, and not serve either side well. The resolution was to build two tracks. At first, this was not a popular suggestion; but once we explained why we wanted to approach the training with these levels, we gained more buy-in from our sponsors. In the end, the company gained a return on investment from this training through improved communications skills, a reduction in project costs, and less scope creep in the execution of the projects.

To avoid either a lack of skilled employees or misaligned training initiatives, I suggest asking a few alignment questions of key stakeholders who are driving the business outcomes.

- What clear business result/outcome are you looking to accomplish?
- Which roles or functions within your organization will be responsible for delivering these results?
- What will the roles or functions need to do differently or better to accomplish the outcome?
- Understanding the desired impact, what is your action plan to support these roles or functions to overcome the gaps?
- How will you clearly confirm whether the action plan is having the intended impact of supporting the business results?

3 Pillar Model

Where I see organizations struggle with strategies for developing people is where the strategies are not implemented holistically throughout the organization. I see three key foundational areas for developing these strategies. I call the combination of these areas my 3 Pillars Model. As you can imagine, if one leg of these pillars is lacking, then you could be facing talent risk, which can easily lead to business risk.

These elements are not new in talent management. However, it is rare to see all three of these pillars working in conjunction with each other to support overall business objectives and strategies. If you are a function or department lead or leading a support function for the business—such as HR or Learning—this model is for everyone and is critical to developing holistic workforce planning strategies across lines of the business. I am not saying this is easy, especially in large, globally distributed organizations. The good news is that there will be technology tools in the near future that will allow us to better understand our talent pool and skills within the organization. I do see the need on all sides to come together and have strategic conversations about how employees support the desired business outcomes. Let's look at the first pillar in the model.

Succession Planning

Your leadership pipeline, also known as succession planning, is critical to executing your strategy. The number one reason employees leave a company is a bad manager. Knowing that your leaders can make or break any given business results, you have to make sure they have the right stuff to succeed. I am not saying we need to invest in traditional, formal training programs of the past. Yes, these are important; however, the speed at which the older generation is retiring is causing a leadership gap. This is not to say that gap cannot be overcome. Not at all! The key is to identify capable leaders who have experience leading teams or who understand foundational knowledge around leading and motivating the people that work for them.

Given some forethought and planning, there is an opportunity to expedite development of newer leaders. This development effort cannot be solely reliant on a week-long training course covering everything a new leader needs to know. That could be a start. I am suggesting a fuller program that applies a targeted, focused approach through which new leaders are exposed to good leadership practices. This type of training might include coaching techniques, emotional intelligence, and leadership styles in conjunction with time to define how these new leaders will incorporate these principles into their leadership paradigm. Leadership training should not be done in a vacuum. As new leaders are testing and learning these new techniques or ideas, they should have opportunities to discuss their progress with more seasoned leaders within the organization. These seasoned leaders can share their experience and coach the new leaders throughout this growth process. This is the future of effective leadership development!

I recently worked with a global healthcare company in building their leadership pipeline. They had a driving business need with new products hitting the market. My team was asked to develop a program to expedite the development of high potential sales representatives and get them ready to step up into management roles within 6–8 months. Oh, by the way, we needed to design, plan, and roll out the program in 1 month! This was a great challenge because most leadership development programs are designed and developed over 3–4 months on average, if not longer, based on organizational needs. What we were being asked to do was truly agile development.

I am happy to say the team stepped up, and we designed a new program in 2 days. I think the key to this stage was focusing on the critical skills needed to be successful in starting out in a new leadership role. We concentrated on four critical skills, around which we built a program. We kicked off the program with a few days of formal, in-person training. The purpose of that training was more about skills-gap development and understanding individual strengths versus a knowledge dump. Don't get me wrong—we did introduce some leadership concepts like coaching, but we were highly selective in what concepts would be introduced at that time.

Another key was pairing the trainees with a seasoned mentor/coach during this period to help them in the process of discovery. The mentors sat in and observed, or role played with them in various scenarios they would encounter as a leader. After each activity, mentors would spend time with their mentees to debrief performance in the given scenario. It was really powerful to see how reflective the learners were and how thoughtfully the mentors guided the process. Everyone was involved and invested in this process. Identifying the right mentors that have a passion around developing people was crucial.

This initial training led into a 6-month virtual program where each potential leader was a self-guided learner. We gave them a high-level roadmap to follow, and they chose which content to dive into to further their development. This included recommended reading lists, videos, digital content, and the like. They also were expected to meet at least once a month with their mentor and their direct manager to discuss these concepts. Each month had a specific topic or theme on which their development focused. We also held a monthly webinar with all the new potential leaders to discuss the theme in more detail or, in some cases, had guest speakers with particular subject matter expertise. This methodology was very well received, and the webinars were highly attended.

To wrap it all up, we brought them back for one last in-person program to expose them to the final foundational skills needed to be a successful leader. For this portion, we brought in executive suite guests to speak to them in a keynote fashion, and these leaders discussed their leadership experiences or provided words of wisdom. At the end of this program, 60% of participants were promoted into leadership roles, sometimes out-maneuvering interim leaders serving in those roles. Because we leveraged internal content, the cost of this type of program was a minimal investment. The biggest cost was the time spent by the mentors and senior leadership team with this program. I would say it was a good use of their time. And, really, at the end of the day, isn't this what great leaders do?

The preceding example is a success story. Unfortunately, they don't all go that way. In interviewing leaders for this book, one of the most common elements mentioned was the selection of leaders and how critical it is to find the right leaders. I have seen the majority of organizations, especially at the front-line leader level, look to promote the highest-performing individual contributors to leadership roles. This is not the best strategy because being a leader involves a totally different mindset and skills. You have to have a passion for developing and coaching others. Just because someone is the top salesperson or has deep technology expertise does not mean that person will be a great leader. In fact, I would say it is highly unlikely that the top salesperson or technical expert will be a good leader. Again, there are very different skill sets required to be successful. I am not saying that these top-performing individuals can't make the transition; many do. But transitioning to leadership requires a shift in expectations and skills. You should not promote high-performing sales or technical leads just to reward them with extra money or a title. There needs to be an alternate career track for those who are perfectly happy being individual contributors. Those individuals can still have growth in their area of expertise without direct reports. Both of these paths should be viable career tracks.

Another way to identify who should be tapped to move into a leadership role is by defining what leadership attributes and values your organization aspires to have or needs. How are leaders expected to develop their people? Do they understand the culture and how to shape that in the organization? New leaders should be willing to develop themselves to understand what motivates their employees to higher levels of performance. Recently I came across a great way to frame the multi-faceted aspects of a leader. It is called the Knowing, Doing, and Being Gap[6], which is based on research compiled at Harvard Business School. The framework emphasizes that it isn't enough for leaders to be exposed to leadership concepts. They need to live and breathe the concepts in their own teams by testing out what works for them. As they test and learn, they will become more successful leaders over time and know when to leverage different tools or techniques as they build their confidence in leading teams. This framework also covers more subtle and nonverbal elements of leadership that speak volumes to teams. It is not always the words you use, but the actions you take that teams pick up on. If you are looking to build out comprehensive leadership development programs, I highly recommend checking out this resource. The researchers have pulled together all the thought leadership in these three areas on how to build out the best programs.

Your organization can also develop predictive analytics for leaders in your organization. These analytics might include the percentage turnover in front-line supervisors, the number of high-potential leaders promoted, and engagement results. These metrics can be shared with key business stakeholders across the organization. Additionally, using leadership forecasting to better understand current and future needs and gaps throughout your organization can be useful. One technique is to use scenario planning to predict leadership gaps. Asking what might happen if certain events happen within your organization can help you to better understand the potential business impact. As an example, how many younger leaders in positions today can be expected to leave if they are not promoted in the next 12 months? To minimize disruption to the business, think about other triggering events that you can use to plan for and mitigate any potential future events. Among the biggest challenges in business today are the shortages of critical role and leadership pipelines. Using some of the techniques described here can give you and your organization an advantage, because you will have developed strategies to address issues should they come to pass. The end game is to have the right leaders in the right place at the right time. This is where planning and execution collide.

Skills Gap Analysis

The pace of change and disruption in the markets is making it difficult to develop training or strategies fast enough to keep up. There is a big focus on upskilling and reskilling the workforce to prepare for or stay current with the changes. Certainly, technology is driving many of these initiatives, with employees needing to learn new processes or technical skills. Artificial intelligence is one technology that is pushing change within organizations, but certainly is not the only driver. So how do you prepare your employees for what is coming so they can continue to be productive? This is where streamlined skills gap analyses will be critical to keep abreast of the changes.

This first step is to really understand what the gap is between the current knowledge, skills, and abilities within your employee pool and what will be needed going forward. Are there certain roles that are lagging behind or that will be impacted the most by the anticipated changes? You can also look at current job descriptions and competency models, if you have them, to identify the gaps. I always recommend interviewing key employees in the impacted roles to really understand the current skill set to identify the gaps. This can be especially valuable if technology will eliminate or enhance certain processes. How will employees be expected to leverage or utilize these technological advances so they have more time to do the valuable tasks your customers want and need? In research conducted on upskilling and reskilling in 2018[7] by the Association for Talent Development, Rob Lauber, Senior VP and Chief Learning Officer at McDonald's, had this insight:

> *Change happens so quickly now that organizations consistently have to reinvent themselves, their offerings, and their products to remain relevant in the marketplace. That means employees have to reinvent, too, by upgrading their skills and learning new ones. Rapid change causes those new skills to become obsolete quickly, so upskilling and reskilling will continue to be critical strategies—for learning and development for business survival.*

Skill enhancement does not always need to be in the form of a formal training program. In fact, research has shown that most employees learn new skills through experiences—through stretch assignments, rotations, or special projects and task forces. We used to call it learning on-the-job or just do it. Experiences do count, but they need to be strategic and aligned not only with the employee's skill gaps, but also the organization's needs. Exposure to how things are done in various parts of the organization can provide fodder and expansive thinking that can be incorporated back into the current role the employee holds. They may even get exposed to career tracks they never considered before, but for which they are actually quite well suited.

A 2016 Gallup report[8] found that nearly twice as many younger employees are willing to job hop as compared to their older colleagues. Much of this trend has been linked to perceived stagnation by this group. They want to be constantly learning new things and adding value to their organizations. If they aren't, they are more willing to walk out the door for another opportunity. What can companies do to avoid upskilling their employees only to lose them to competitors? Companies can invest in artificial intelligence to monitor workforce analytics. IBM is leveraging Watson in 2018 and has developed a bot to analyze employee performance and growth. The bot is called Watson Career Coach, and it can predict patterns of flight risk by comparing data trends within IBM. It can also serve as an AI-assisted talent adviser helping provide employees guided career suggestions—from reskilling to promotions—by looking at colleagues' trends and career trajectories. These are future abilities of the HR and Talent Development functions coming soon.

Another trend that has some promise is partnering with educational institutions to create customized certification tracks on specific programs and foundational skills. In partnership with the organization, colleges, universities, and technical/vocational schools are building specialized programs to meet current and future needs. There are two points of entry back to the organization in this model. Either current employees attend these programs to reskill or upskill within the organization, or students partner with organizations to spend some time working on special projects to gain real-world experience and exposure to the organization. Many of these types of partnerships lead to a low-risk pipeline of new or refreshed talent for the organization. These types of programs have arisen as a fluid model of keeping skills fresh versus obtaining a degree and then never having to "officially" learn anything more. In the future of work, the jobs of today will not look or feel like the jobs in 10 or 15 years from now.

Within organizations, we tend to think of coaching and mentorship as ways to learn from others. As a leader, coaching can be a powerful tool if done right. Coaching is listening and guiding in the spirit of helping to develop someone else. It can get confused with feedback, which is more telling. There are mixed views on how you should provide feedback, especially in the context of annual performance reviews, which have gotten a bad name, for good reason, especially if feedback is happening only once per year. I have found in working with clients around the world that coaching is a better approach, because the one being coached reflects and provides solutions that lead to more ownership of solving the problem or overcoming challenges.

A good example of strategic mentorship programs that are having an impact was demonstrated at a conference I attended. The company is a large, global facilities management organization that recently adopted a different approach to mentorship. In a pilot program, the company paired up senior-level managers with up-and-coming talent (new managers) to not only develop needed skill sets, but also to have the senior leaders share their experiences. The mentees found the program very engaging and relatable. The senior managers, by sharing their stories, were open to relating lessons learned to help demonstrate the impact of decisions they made during their careers. The program was so successful that the company's employee engagement scores rose with the new managers significantly. By the end of the pilot, new managers were lining up to get into the next cohort to participate. It was seen as advantageous and also allowed for exposure to senior leaders who otherwise not be accessible.

Taking the program a step further, the senior leaders are now receiving reverse mentoring, which means the senior leaders are assuming a mentee role, and the new managers are mentoring those leaders on technology or new ways to do business that they have been exposed to. Reverse mentoring can be tricky, as you can imagine, but it was successful because the first senior leader to go through it was the president of that particular region. The president's participation sent a signal to the rest of his team that if he can do it, they can too. I believe you have to have this level of engagement and support for this type of arrangement to be successful or even to get off the ground.

One last trend I am seeing in organizations is a move away from a traditional classroom-based model—one where the facilitator/teacher/sage on the stage is communicating the knowledge to the learners. It is no longer acceptable for training to be in the form of sitting and listening to a lecture for hours on end, and you will notice a downturn in your course evaluations if you continue to instruct this way. What is more acceptable is a blended, facilitated style. The lecturer may still be guiding the learners, but in shorter blocks of time, usually no more than 15 minutes. It is more important for learners to discuss and work through the content than to be told about a particular model or how to use it. That can all be learned independently. The focus now is on application-based instruction, which means more time is spent on how a learner will use this new information and start to apply it back on the job, and the approach to learning is much more collaborative and team-based. I also am starting to see tools that allow learners to consume content at their own pace through personalized learning tracks. Learners find it more relevant and impactful as they move through the content based on the experience or skills they bring to the course. This type of tool is in early stages, but I am guessing we will be utilizing this technology more in the future, especially outside a classroom.

As you can see, there are many options in the development of employees within your organization that actually are very cost effective. In a world where great talent is hard to come by, don't you think it is worth your time and effort to develop your employees? Who knows? They might surprise you!

In both of these first two Pillars described, a portion of the solution will always lie in hiring from the outside. Organizations and you, as a leader, spend a lot of time finding the right candidate to join the organization. It is up to you and your HR team to decide the right mix of internal leadership development and upskilling required based on business needs. I would say a smaller portion should come from outside because of the effect it has on the organizational culture. You may also need an infusion of outside perspectives to help boost innovation and creativity. These are good reasons to look outside. My word of caution is to proceed carefully. With a little care and feeding, you may have just what you need internally. As always, it is a balance we maintain, and only you really know the right answers.

Performance Needs

The last leg of the pillar is performance management. I know many organizations that still use a traditional annual performance review model. At the beginning of the year, the employees outline their goals for the year. No one looks at them again until your manager or HR reminds you do a self-review of what you achieved compared to the goals you outlined months earlier. This approach is generally viewed as a painful, time-consuming process that has little value. This is not the performance management I am referencing in this pillar.

What I am referring to is a performance-based model that is ongoing and more holistic for the organization. In this model, the organizational environment is analyzed for potential gaps in performance, such as in management and systems. With this mindset, we look closely at organizations and departments to uncover areas for improvement. We start with where value is being created through goals and outcomes. The goals and outcomes are tied nicely with the strategic plan, so we look at areas that are important to the organization to uncover any metrics or measures that are not being achieved. Some examples include gaining new customers, reducing turnover, and increasing customer retention. Once we know which goals the organization is not meeting, we work to understand and identify what processes, tasks, and roles are tied to them. At the end of the day, we focus on the people who are completing the tasks for that role so we can dive deeper into what is influencing their environment and how can we improve it.

Processes are an inherent aspect of the model. What processes are tied directly to the outcomes and goals? Does the organization have a process and, if so, is it documented? Do people follow the processes or do they go around them? Processes are critical to understand, especially when rolling out new technology and systems.

With regard to technology, what systems are these roles using, particularly to achieve the targeted outcomes and goals? After identifying what automated tools are being used, you can ask the employees how they are interacting with them and whether they find them valuable in their role. Because we still have generations in the workforce that didn't grow up with abundant technology or computers, it is good to understand their comfort level in using these tools. Don't assume that everyone is comfortable or savvy in utilizing tech. Hopefully these tools are making everyone's lives easier, but many times we find they are not designed with the end user in mind. Looking to the future, any new technology has to factor in the human interface, how it will be used, and the value it is creating in meeting the end goals and outcomes.

We have already explored the value of coaching and feedback in this chapter, but now our lens is on how effectively managers are providing timely feedback or coaching to their teams. What if they truly have a performance issue? How do they go about tackling that challenge? Do they wait until the end of the year at the performance review? There should be no surprises in talking to your employees at performance review time. It does not serve you or the employee well to wait. We also look at accountability on teams. Are managers setting performance expectations and holding their teams accountable? And beyond providing feedback or coaching, do the employees understand what is expected of them from their manager? The communication needs to go two ways, and transparency is key.

The next piece of the performance puzzle is rewards and recognition. This includes more than just benefits and compensation, although those are important when bringing on new employees and being competitive. I am talking about recognizing the day-to-day contributions of teams and leaders. For instance, are there programs within the organization to recognize good work? If so, how do they work? Can employees recognize one another, or does recognition come only from the managers? Are the programs being used? Another question I like to ask is, are we providing incentives for the right behaviors? One negative I have witnessed is when top performers are rewarded with more work when they do a good job or hit their goals early. Think about what signal this sends to the rest of the team. Do you suppose some team members will slide back and take longer because they know their manager will offload another task or project to the high performers on the team? Is that okay? No judgment, just a question. It might be a way to weed out low performers, but I would have to ask, to what detriment?

I find that work conditions are rarely discussed in organizations, but they are very valuable to understand. When exploring work conditions within an organization, I ask employees about the leadership team as a whole, usually the individuals at the top of an organization. Culture and politics are the key drivers I am trying to uncover. All organizations have these elements. In fact, organizational values are usually posted on company websites and on the walls at work. Do these values resonate, or is it just artwork? Are we holding ourselves accountable to these values? Leadership plays a huge role in following through on words and action. The strength of the leadership team is usually a sign of a good or challenging culture.

The bottom line is, as an employee, would you follow your leadership team?

Closely related to performance needs are key performance indicators, or as they are commonly known, KPIs. You would be surprised how many companies don't have them. Or if they do, they measure too much in one area or fail to measure things that will provide insight into low performance. How will I know whether individual performance will lead to organizational performance? Busywork does not translate into business results. Do we understand those key tasks or processes that produce the desired outcomes and ultimately help us meet our strategic goals for the organization? In working with those who are closest to the task or process, you can better understand how to measure the desired outcomes.

As you can see, by working through the 3 pillars of this model, you can get a better view of the talent in the organization and develop clear strategies to address what needs attention. Much of what I have described here is not new, but the value lies in pulling everything together and thinking more at a systemic and strategic level for the organization. It is not enough to consider any one factor on its own anymore. These types of discussions need to happen at the highest level to craft a targeted plan of action and to keep on top of how the organization is trending against its strategic goals. This is truly macro-level organizational development and enhancement.

Unfortunately, most organizations fail to look at their talent pools as a whole. There are many factors that affect performance and execution of any given strategy. By understanding where your current department/function stands within the whole of the organization, you can devise strategies for how each team member will support the organization's goals. Beyond technology, people are the driving force behind your organization's success. It is time for organizations to foster this resource with more care and feeding because doing so will reap benefits for many years to come.

Key Takeaways:

✓ Company strategies need to be communicated well and understood at all levels. Strategies need to be in a clear line of sight at each level. The execution of strategies tends to get stuck somewhere in the middle levels of organizations. Find ways to engage employees at all levels.

✓ Understanding where your talent lies within your organization and identifying the gaps in skills or knowledge in relation to the strategies will be a key differentiator for competitive organizations.

✓ Use the 3 Pillars Model to support overall business results and deliver the outcomes rooted in strategies.

✓ Selection and preparation of future leaders is an ongoing investment within successful companies. Don't leave promotions to chance and hope for the best. Help to provide a foundation of skills that leaders need to be successful at all phases of their career.

✓ Invest smartly in talent skill gaps. By identifying what needs to change, you can create a baseline of what skills employees have and what evolving skills will be needed in the near future. Don't wait to figure this out in the end and expect success. New knowledge and skills take time and practice.

✓ Think about ways to identify skill gaps in order to fulfill or build needed skills in the workplace. Gaps could be filled through outside sources, mentoring programs, or just-in-time learning on specific skills.

✓ By uncovering the root cause of performance gaps among employees, we can develop organizational strategies to mitigate issues and pave the way for obtaining the strategic goals.

Building Agility for the
Future Workforce

There is a lot of talk about machine learning and artificial intelligence (AI) and how it will take over jobs in the near future. As we enter this accelerated AI world, there are many considerations around how these new systems are implemented. In this chapter, I will explore ways to involve employees in building out these systems, along with the necessary leadership capabilities that will be needed to be successful at implementing these solutions.

Topics covered in this chapter include:

- Myths about artificial intelligence
- Coexisting with artificial intelligence
- The global talent pool
- Key soft skills
- Positive change
- Transitioning skills and roles
- Organizational structure
- Defining new business models

Myths about Artificial Intelligence

Before we start devising strategies on how to bring technology into your organization, let's dispel some AI myths.

Myth #1: AI will take over jobs.

The first myth is around jobs. The big question that I get the most: Are AI systems going to take over all the jobs? The quick answer is, No! Will it impact many jobs? The answer is, Yes! Think about AI as taking over certain tasks within job roles, such as researching case law for precedence in a pending lawsuit, creating profit and loss statements, or performing rote tasks that have established processes. All of these can be done better, faster, and more efficiently by technology than a human. In the example of researching case law, a human conducting research to prepare for a lawsuit will take an average of weeks, whereas AI can conduct the research in hours as it pulls from its vast database.

A recent article in *Fast Company* claimed that the AI software *Arterys* can diagnose heart problems from an MRI scan in 15 seconds as compared to 30 minutes for the average professional human analyst to produce the same results.[9] This is one of many examples of technology being utilized in various fields.

This advanced technology means we will be dealing with job transformation in many industries. In my research, I came across this estimate of certain job categories that will be impacted by AI.[10] The percentages represent the percent of today's tasks AI will be able to do within those job roles.

- Management, business, and financial—64% by 2020
- Sales and related—52% by 2020
- Transportation and material moving—41% by 2020

So, as you can see, AI is impacting a cross section of job categories and will touch all levels in organizations. It is too early to know the extent of job displacement and other impacts; but assuming a utopian mindset, we can expect new job categories in the future that haven't been invented yet. If you think about the last 30 years, I would say that technologies have had a major impact; but going forward, the changes will be expedited and much more noticeable. To avoid a dystopian society, our machine learning creations need to work synergistically with humans to create more meaningful work. It will mean a shift from mundane or highly manual tasks to those that create value for customers in new and exciting ways. It is what we do with these new technologies and data sources that is the most important, especially when we aim to delight customers and stakeholders. A recent *Wall Street Journal* article described the future impact of advanced technology: "It affects every industry, not just manufacturing, logistics or transportation, and is unique in the degree to which it is affecting white-collar as well as blue-collar workers. We're either witnessing the end of work as we know it or 'merely' a profound transformation of what jobs humans do. Either way, the economic and political ramifications are likely to be on par with the impact of the past 50 years of outsourcing and globalization."[11] The final takeaway from this myth is that machines will not take over all of our jobs, at least not completely. But how we spend our time will most certainly be changing in this new environment.

Myth #2: AI can make rational decisions.

This brings me to the second myth in this evolution, which is the extent to which artificial intelligence can rationalize and make decisions. Let's be clear, as fantastic as the algorithms are now and in the near future, AI is not cognizant in the same way as a human is. This means while AI can digest tons of data in a short period of time, the software is looking for patterns, which is something the software is better at. Though AI programs may seem to be thinking, they are really just processing algorithms. That is, the AI software cannot go beyond what the algorithm can do to perform additional tasks unless the algorithm and tasks have been connected somehow. As an example of this, AI software cannot make dinner. Think about how many steps there are and what could go wrong in the preparation. There are small, but important adjustments in this task that cannot be easily programmed. These types of decisions and needed adjustments are still in the realm of human capacity.

In your organization, I am sure you can think of many tasks that cannot be solved easily with an algorithm. I worked with a client recently on this journey to implement intelligent software. We were creating a form that would capture customer data all in one place so that employees could more easily quote on the creation of specialized products. Previously, employees were capturing this information via their business email, and it wasn't in a standardized format or stored anywhere collectively. The process was becoming unruly, and the time spent in gathering this data manually took a large percentage of their time away from value-added activities in working with their customers. The department was not able to sustain their grow plans without hiring a lot more employees. Customers valued the personal relationships they built with employees, and chasing down emails was taking away from key relationship building as conversations where much more transactional in nature. In other words, by creating an automated form, that time was given back to the employees. The automated data collection form streamlined the company's process and reduced the need for so much email communication. Over time, the data collected can allow for more meaningful conversations around strategic opportunities. The data also can reveal competitive landscape trends that can help their customers grow their businesses in high-demand areas.

No system can build these relationships with customers. Systems can reveal areas of opportunity for our businesses, but we are the ones who need to take action on those opportunities. The data collection is certainly key, but the real value in the future is what you do strategically with that knowledge. That is what differentiates humans from machines. The machines collect the data and can recognize patterns. In turn, the humans will need to make sense of this information to decide which direction or strategies to put in place to be competitive.

Myth #3: Technology (AI) implementation is easy.

The last myth I will explore is about implementation of AI within organizations. Though the technology may be easy to use, the success of its implementation depends on the people. As leaders, we need to be thoughtful about how the technology will impact our organizations. As you might be experiencing and feeling, employees are fearful of the future of their work. If we are driving employees away from performing standard processes, they might wonder, "well, what will I be doing?" Implementation requires a major mindset shift for most employees. Different skill sets will be demanded, such as soft skills for focusing on the customer experience and nurturing those relationships. Jobs will be more about solving problems and being creative.

I think there are opportunities to partner with departments like human resources, training, and organizational development to develop strategies for transitioning employees and preparing them for the skills of the future. In organizations I've researched that have started implementing AI solutions, their biggest lesson learned is that employee transition and reskilling need to happen earlier than you think—and before the actual transition happens. Employees need to be involved in creating this new reality and to understand what makes sense for the machines to do and what roles will remain with them.

If you are a leader in Human Resources or other functions that support employees, you have an opportunity to be more strategic by moving away from processes and tasks yourselves. Our organizations are going to need HR support now more than ever to help pull through these transformations successfully. HR can help our leaders identify the skills and competencies needed ahead of time. This will allow us to be transparent with our employees and clear about the future needs of the organization. Later in this chapter, I discuss ways to help our leaders craft the business model of the future to support the organization in this transformational period.

"Financial capital is easy, but human capital is much harder. I need talent strategies that get me the talent I need now."
Senior leader at Allstate Insurance,
Claim Strategy & Innovation

Coexisting with Artificial Intelligence

Now that we have explored the top myths about AI coming into our lives, let's take some time to better understand what artificial intelligence is and its applications.

We are already in the midst of a transformation to artificial intelligence and machine learning for creating better customer experiences. Think about your Netflix® or Amazon experiences. I often wonder how those applications know exactly what to offer up to me. By leveraging the Internet for shopping or searching for the right show to watch on a Sunday evening, you are creating a data trail that starts to tell a story about you and what you like or not. If you look at companies at the forefront of this transformation, you will find Facebook®, Amazon, Netflix, and Google™ (also referred to as FANG). Think about the amount of data they have collected from you over the last few years. They have refined their AI solutions (they have a network of AI solutions working together seamlessly in the background) to the point that they are quite sophisticated. But this did not happen overnight; they've been testing and learning what works over time. They've been willing to take risks on a global scale in order to learn. I am not saying that we, as leaders, will be working with AI at that level of sophistication, but it is important to note that AI is here, and we need to figure out how to coexist with it.

I point this out because those organizations that embrace AI and start to strategically think about best uses will have a competitive advantage over those who lag or wait. So, the question is, where do we start? I would suggest starting small and testing specific processes that are ideal for automation. We all have opportunities within our organizations to create a better customer experience or to improve the backend processes that fall under operations, finance, and administration. The key is to focus on outcomes. How will the customer or stakeholder experience be enhanced by automating this process or procedure? Alternatively, think about areas that could be automated with AI or bots that could capture important customer data to better reveal insights about customers. Just like my earlier example about capturing customer requests automatically versus manually, automating data collection processes allows you and your employees to spend more of your valuable time and effort on building relationships with customers at a deeper level than before. Those leaders who have already started down this path are beginning to see employee engagement surge as they perform more meaningful work. This is the power, if done right.

The Global Talent Pool

Another piece of the puzzle yet to be revealed is the global implications of research and development efforts in machine learning. All of the major economies of the world are investing in this type of research. In fact, China is on track to spend more on research and development in this area than the United States in a recent report from the National Science Foundation. I point this out because it will have an impact on the war for talent, as highlighted in this section of the news release from that report:

> *Higher education provides the advanced work*
> *skills needed in an increasingly knowledge-intensive*
> *global economy. According to the most recent*

estimates, the U.S. awarded the largest number of S&E [Science & Engineering] doctoral degrees (40,000) of any country, followed by China (34,000), Russia (19,000) Germany (15,000), the United Kingdom (14,000), and India (13,000). In contrast, the U.S. lags in bachelor's level degrees. India earned 25% of the more than 7.5 million awarded S&E bachelor's level degrees in 2014, followed closely by China (22%), the EU (12%), and the U.S. (10%). Nearly half of all degrees awarded in China are in S&E fields. Since 2000, the number of S&E bachelor's degrees awarded in China has gone up by 300%.

Over the past twenty years, students have become more internationally mobile and countries increasingly compete for them as potential recruits for the S&E workforce. International student numbers in the U.S. dropped between the fall of 2016 and the fall of 2017, with the largest declines seen at the graduate level in computer science (13% decline) and engineering (8% decline). International students account for over 57% of graduate enrollments in computer sciences and engineering in the U.S. These students are a critical component of the U.S. workforce in these high demand fields. Seventy nine percent of foreign doctoral graduate students choose to stay and work in the U.S. upon completion of their degree.[12]

We need to think about our talent pool from a global perspective. We will be competing for the same top talent worldwide. If you open your mind to this, you may think about recruiting from a different lens. Why would a potential employee choose your company over many others around the world? It is becoming even more important to show potential hires why your company is the best choice.

Key Soft Skills

Let's talk about our current employees and the impact on their jobs in the near future. How can we prepare out teams and employees for this change? We will need to spend time reskilling and upskilling. What do these terms mean, and how do they differ from each other? For reskilling, we look at job roles and what will change. We need to be clear and transparent about what each role will be doing and, more importantly, what those roles will no longer be doing. To facilitate reskilling, we will be helping with reframing jobs and may expand certain areas, like customer service, but in a more strategic way and not as tactical. In upskilling, we are talking about skills and competencies that an employee may not have yet but will need to develop to be successful in the future. Some examples of upskilling that I am seeing are soft skills. I've been asked many times what skills we should be focusing on to better support employees or prepare them for the future workforce (if they are in college or university now). Here are eight critical soft skills needed now and in the near future:

1. **Critical thinking ability**. This is key for making decisions with the massive amount of data being collected and compiled.
2. **Data analysis**. This skill goes hand in hand with the previous one; we need to be able to make sense of data because we are all data scientists now.
3. **Creativity**. Being able to see beyond what is in front of us and create new realities will be essential. Much more teamwork with a diversity of perspectives is also paving the way forward.
4. **Innovation**. This skill is tied closely with the previous one, but the nuance is taking ideas and putting them into reality—not just seeing the opportunity but also making it happen.

5. **Strategic thinking**. Because the tactical tasks will be better handled by machines, we will be expected to think more in big picture terms.

6. **Growth mindset**. This skill calls for being open and flexible to new ideas, willing to take risks and experience failure while learning, and taking the learning and making ourselves more resilient.

7. **Curiosity**. Constantly learning new things and being open to new ideas are the ways of the future.

8. **Change management ability**. Helping ourselves and others through rapid and changing environments will be an important skill. Our focus must be on possibilities and not deficit; we must maintain positivity.

Positive Change

Our challenge with this new future of work is creating a synergistic relationship between technology and people, where people are excited about changes and advances. I want to elaborate a bit more on the last skill in the preceding list—change management ability—because it is important as we go down this path together. I am sure many of us have been through poorly managed change programs in our careers. In research conducted by Willis Towers Watson,[13] a leading global advisory firm focused on talent, their findings showed that 75% of change efforts were not sustained long-term within organizations. If we have that much failure incorporating AI and machine learning systems, we are in big trouble. This statistic shows that we need a different mindset when working toward our future organizations.

We need a shift away from burning platforms and rallying the troops without understanding the implications of how this change will impact our organizations and beyond. In large-scale change such as this, we need to think more at a macro level versus a micro level. How do we elevate our efforts to think beyond our immediate sphere of influence and knowledge to benefit from a much larger outreach? By tapping into and elevating human potential, we can drive change at the scale of the whole organization.

Recently, research around the positive aspects of change in our lives has come to the forefront and is showing very positive results in just shifting our mindset from a deficit or loss mode to growth and positivity. If we think about change in our lives, we've dealt with it regularly from moving schools to moving for a career opportunity. We are malleable creatures and can flex with our environments. It is how we have survived and gotten to the top of the food chain.

One way to tap into positive psychology is to leverage individuals' strengths. Many leaders are aware of recent leadership philosophies shifting from working on weaknesses to maximizing strengths. Working with what we do best allows us to demonstrate our best work and feel good about it. This is the tie back to positivity. When we get to flex our strengths, our organizations are getting the best work out of us. It is a win-win situation as all parties are satisfied. This does not mean you always get to work only in your areas of strength. Let's be clear. The majority of your time is spent on tasks that leverage your individual strengths. The cool thing is, we all have strengths of different varieties, so the possibilities are endless. Another benefit of focusing on strengths is increased employee engagement, according to Gallup, the organization that developed StrengthsFinder [now CliftonStrengths®].[14] Now, imagine working and leading in an organization that values this type of mentality, and you are guaranteed to increase creativity and collaboration across the whole of the organization.

Another aspect of positive change effort is in the framing. The way we approach a change can have a negative or limiting impact from the effort. In other words, if you frame the change effort as a problem or something to fix, you are enabling the problem to be the focus of the change effort. But if you shift your thinking to something more expansive, then you enable the possibilities of what could be, and thereby look beyond the problem to opportunities. Another big reason change efforts fail is because employees feel that change is happening to them, so they resist. A more inclusive and enlightened viewpoint is involving all of the various stakeholder groups, internally and externally, to help shape the future that will open up and inspire everyone to work together for a higher purpose. This might seem impossible or outrageous, but there are many organizations that have used this framing to bring hundreds of stakeholders and employees together with great results. Their employees were excited and energized by what the future might hold for them. I don't know about you, but this seems like a much more exciting way to lead people through change efforts.

Transitioning Skills and Roles

Now, I'd like to elaborate on impacts on skill set and roles. As I pointed out earlier in this chapter, identifying and recognizing impacts to employee's skills and roles will be key during these transitions. As a leader, you will need to be able to articulate the potential impacts with your team or have them work through it together. Where is the transition point of machine to human? What skills or tasks are no longer needed for a human to do? I believe our skill sets will be fluid during this time, and the bar will continually be raised as we build more and more machine capabilities. According to a report published by *Harvard Business Review,* [15]

Redeployment and reskilling of existing workers is a massive challenge that societies must confront. Today, for example, America spends huge amounts educating kids but spends very little re-educating adults.

With this technology wave, there is also a new opportunity to partner with academic institutions in ways we haven't before. As global corporations are struggling to keep up, so are educational programs. I can't even imagine trying to develop curriculum for students in this day and age knowing that it will change by the time they graduate in a few years. I've talked to many professors about this challenge and believe that we need to rethink our traditional mindset around advanced degrees and how we obtain them. How do we stay current with the vast amounts of data and change to come in the future? We currently think about subject matter for degrees in the present. But will that be good enough for the future needs of organizations? What does that relationship look like?

I don't have the answers, but I think we have a great opportunity to rethink how we educate our future workforce. Creating a collaboration of educational institutions and organizations, we can define programs together that will be of benefit to both. What does this look like? Maybe not a 4-year degree for an undergraduate program, but it might be a mix of classroom and team collaboration with apprenticeships in companies or organizations to solve problems or work on specific challenges. I see this system as a win-win as students get to apply and utilize new knowledge right away and organizations get to observe potential new talent and get things done. There are many ways we can evolve all of our organizations to better fit the new reality coming our way.

As with all areas of the business, human resources departments will be enhanced with predictive analytics solutions. Leaders and talent support organizations (talent development, organizational development, and human resources) will be able to collect, analyse and run dashboards of information on the talent within the organization. This will allow better decision making and planning for the future. We will be able to better forecast what will be needed to fill the gaps within the current talent pool.

Organizational Structure

We can also look at how to pull together the best teams for a particular project and to tap into diverse perspectives and experiences. I also believe that the way we are structured as organizations now will not serve us well in the future. So, I imagine our organizational structures will be much more fluid and move further away from the current hierarchical structure. We are already seeing these types of predictive HR analytic systems in the market, but we are just beginning to understand the power and capabilities of these systems to help improve productivity and employee satisfaction.

In a recent article in *Harvard Business Review*,[16] this type of teaming and organizational structure was discovered at a large Chinese appliance maker. This company has formed what they call Microenterprises (ME) within their organization. Each of these MEs has an average of 10 to 15 employees. The types of MEs include market-facing, R&D (new product innovation), and "nodes" (design, manufacturing, and human resources) to support the market-facing teams. How does this work? Well, each ME has goals that are tied to internal and external benchmarks for growth and opportunity. The "node" MEs are internally contracted by the other two types of ME groups. The "node" MEs use service-level agreements with other ME groups, and the other ME groups can "fire" or renegotiate a contract with a "node" if they don't receive the level of service needed to support their goals. Additionally, they can contract with outside resources if they deem fit. This is where I think it gets interesting because these "node" MEs are not just competing internally to support their organizations, but also need to be cognizant of external service providers to stay competitive and offer the best ways to support these teams. This example provides a new look at ways to structure organizations of the future.

You might ask what the implications to leadership and their role are in this type of organization. From a leadership perspective it will be imperative to drive the vision and empower teams to derive business value by adopting AI in areas of the organization where it makes sense. As I have mentioned in other parts of this book, leaders need to shift their mindset on how decisions are made and at what level. It will be impossible to deliver business results while holding onto decision making power. A recent *Harvard Business Review* report emphasized this point:

> *Decisions in organizations have often been made based on "HiPPO"—the highest paid person's opinion. But data-driven organizations have a different culture and a different dialogue; decisions are driven by data, analysis, and conversations that reflect everyone's perspective, without regard to level or position.*[17]

In addition, the report emphasized that there will be a shortage of talent—not enough people with AI and data analytics skills. Companies will need to think about how to strategically deploy these scarce resources in a way that makes sense to support and drive AI initiatives. There will also be a need for employees who are good at translating technology and business requirements and can offer feasible solutions for day-to-day operations. Traditionally, these positions were called Business Analyst, but people in this role will also now need to think about how the end-user within the organization digests and interprets the data served up. At the end of the day, I see three pools of talent. One pool will have the AI and data scientists who are developing AI solutions (think more programming, data training, data programming, and algorithms). The next group will be the converters, who have a view of the business problem they are trying to solve and who also understand enough of the technology to work with the data scientists. Last will be the end users in the business, who need to make decisions based on the data being gathered and presented to them. Each of these groups will play a critical role in the success or failure of implementing AI into the organization.

At the end of the day, all leaders within the organization are going to need a working knowledge of AI and data analytics. To what extent will depend on your level within the organization. At the highest levels, your knowledge won't need to be extensive, but you will at least need to know the basics of these topics and how they can enhance your business. For those leaders who are closer to the customer, you will need much more in-depth knowledge in these areas because you will be driving the changes and influencing stakeholder groups to adopt those changes.

When Peter Senge described a learning organization in his book *The Fifth Discipline* back in 1990, I am sure he could not see this far into the future. Nonetheless, his work is still very insightful for today's AI environment. As he outlined what a learning organization entails, he really was describing future teams and organizations. It has taken 30 years for his vision of organizations to come true, but I believe it is highly relevant now more than ever. Just to summarize, a learning organization is made up of five disciplines, which he outlines in detail in the book. The key competencies needed for this type of organization to thrive are personal mastery, mindset or mental modes, building shared vision, team learning, and thinking systematically. By leveraging each of these competencies, organizations would be able to problem solve within complex systems or organizations. I think we all would agree that most of our lives inside and out of our organizations are complex. My recommendation to you is to revisit Peter Senge's book on this topic and think about how to apply it to your work.

Defining New Business Models

Another need I am seeing in this transformation is to define new business models for all industries. Our current organizational structures and systems will not serve us well in the future. As these new models are yet to be defined, I would suggest utilizing models that can help surface some new ideas. One way to do this is through design thinking. It is not a new methodology, but I certainly see how it could help organizations define models that will serve them better as they move into the unknown. Design thinking was originally founded in the 1960s by industrial and product design teams to evolve better products for the end user.

Those teams defined a set of design principles to develop better products and services.

> *Design thinking is now known as a creative-problem solving approach designers use to create new values that are different and create positive impact.*[18]

Another definition that describes it well is:

> *Design thinking is applied as an umbrella term for multi-disciplinary, human-centered projects that involve research and rapid ideation.*[19]

To create AI sustainability for the future, design thinking models can provide the structure to test and learn from possible future scenarios. The model is not problem focused in its orientation, so the potential scenarios are unlimited. Typical questions are "How might we . . .?" and "What if anything were possible?" The idea is to think about a prospective future that hasn't happened yet. The framing of this new way forward is key to an organization's success. Teams need to look beyond the problem. By co-creating the future with your stakeholders, you open up new possibilities and seek ideas from internal and external sources. Also, because you are not focused on fixing a problem, your mindset is in a discovery mode, allowing you to think more expansively.

Once you have a few good working models or products, it is time to test and learn from what is working and what can be improved. This whole process is iterative, so don't think you have to get it right the first time. In fact, by putting the models or products out there, you will learn a lot about your stakeholder groups, and they will feel a part of the process and solution in moving forward. In this mode, build on what is working well and redefine what is not. A great analogy for this process is to think like jazz musicians. When playing jazz, musicians are listening and improvising as they are playing. No matter how many times they have played together or played a particular piece, the music is always different depending on how each person plays in that moment and where they are feeling the emphasis. At the end of the process, the musicians will start to define the value of what they have pulled together and, because they have tested it along the way, they will know it is a better solution than rolling it out and hoping it works. By working through the process of the change and making adjustments, your organization is creating a new reality, and the old paradigms just slip away. Moreover, because employees are involved in this process, resistance is kept to a minimum. The change is co-created, so employees are invested and don't feel they are being forced to change. They are the change!

The term VUCA was originally coined by the U.S. military in the mid-1990s to describe the post-cold-war disruption. The acronym stands for:

V for **Volatility:** The nature of change in the world today.

U for **Uncertainty**: The inability to predict future events.

C for **Complexity**: No clear relationship between cause and effect; multiple parts/systems involved.

A for **Ambiguity**: A world where relationships are unclear; lack of precision; facing unknowns.

VUCA became popular in mainstream, corporate business talk around the 2008 financial crisis. It is certainly relevant in today's world and probably describes how most of us are feeling in the face of so much change due to technological advances.

We don't know what the next 5 to 10 years will hold for our organizations. This is true across industries, countries, and political lines. We will learn a lot over the coming years about what works well and what to toss. The next wave of technology will be expansive in its reach. As leaders in our organizations, we need to be prepared to step up and guide in this VUCA world— to provide the true north for our organizations. Nobody is saying it will be easy, but we have to be willing to take some risks. Otherwise, our organizations will fall behind and become obsolete, like it or not.

> *"In a world that's changing really quickly, the only strategy that is guaranteed to fail is not taking risks."*
> Mark Zuckerberg,
> CEO of Facebook

Key Takeaways:

✓ Artificial intelligence will impact jobs. It is uncertain to what extent the impact will be felt; but unlike other technology evolutions, this one will be felt at all levels of organizations and across industries.

✓ AI will not take over more complex customer interactions. AI is better at recognizing patterns than humans are, so it is best used for repetitive tasks that require lots of data analysis.

✓ When beginning AI projects, start to think early about the people transitions and the new skills needed to be successful. You can't start too early in developing these talent strategies.

✓ Investment in future talent and AI research and development from countries such as India and China are outpacing the United States. Top talent from around the world will be in high demand, and it will get increasingly harder for U.S. firms to compete.

✓ There are eight critical skills that every employee will need over the next 10 years.

✓ Leaders need to manage change at a macro-level across the organization if the new technology has any success in helping the organization be more competitive. New change methods that focus on strengths of people and organizations versus a deficit philosophy will be key in shifting paradigms.

✓ Reskilling and redeployment of employees will be critical to deliver any real value that technology provides.

✓ Organizational structures will be changing to accommodate the lack of skilled workers and top talent in technology.

Decision making and power will need to be pushed to the lowest level, as close to the customer as possible.

✓ Organizations can use design thinking principles in developing new reporting structures and determining how the work should be organized. By asking "what if?" and involving employees in the process, you will have a higher level of investment for success.

Developing Talent in a Fast-Changing Environment

Technology is impacting our everyday lives in ways we could not even imagine a couple years ago. Work has become more and more complex and more difficult to keep up with. There are so many moving targets, it is difficult to know which information to pay attention to. Where do we start to address the growing skills gap in our workforce? It is estimated that more than 50% of job openings are left unfilled due to a shortage in workers with the right skills. Interestingly, though, there are millions of unemployed looking for work. How did this gap grow so large, and what can we do about it? While consulting for many large organizations around the world, I have noticed a trend of employers upping the bar on what a qualified candidate needs in order to be considered for a job. High expectations work well if you have a large pool of people to choose from. But when unemployment is low or there is a shortage of those with certain skill sets, this strategy does not work.

I suggest a reframing of the mindset around talent within organizations and new hires you want to bring in. What I am talking about is understanding what baseline is needed for any given job and building from there. Organizations have become accustomed to asking for everything upfront—proven skills within the individual's current role so that the transition allows for the employee to hit the ground running without a lot of investment from the company beyond onboarding. What if instead we better understood the skill sets of our workforce or potential workforce and identified and defined a specific plan of action tailored to the gaps within an employee's knowledge base that allows that person to learn and grow on the job? We have failed to own this part of our positions in developing the skills and knowledge of our organizations. Instead of talent management (which is passive and reactive), I am suggesting we focus on *talent enhancement.*

By viewing the needs of the organization and looking at the current skill sets of employees, the skills and knowledge needed for each role within the organization can be developed. We can create tailored programs and professional development based on the individual needs of each employee. As leaders of the organization, it is in our best interest to understand how to develop our people and to provide them the learning opportunities needed to grow and challenge them. There are many ways to do this, but I have found a key mix of development opportunities and leveraging the current knowledge base within the organization is the best strategy for continually building new insights and skills that will help make your organization competitive and be successful.

Topics covered in this chapter include:

- Knowledge management
- Employees learning from others
- Personalized learning
- Employee productivity
- Artificial intelligence and the future of work
- The talent progression

Knowledge Management

I interviewed leadership expert Jonathan Silk, former West Point instructor and CEO of Bridge 3, a leading team and organizational development firm. He introduced me to the concept of generational leadership, which he learned in his military service.

> *If you are a leader that has an idea of generational leadership as a vision, you would have an eye for the future and develop me with future generations in mind, knowing that I would go on to develop others and they would go on to develop others down the line. Those people may never meet you, but they feel your presence and influence through previous leaders. As I develop leaders today, I think about the responsibility for leadership, not just the ones in front of you, but maybe five generations down the line. It is all about building sustainability in your organization. It's really about good leader talent development in my opinion.*

Knowledge management is the first strategy for developing talent. What will the mix of opportunities look like within your organization? Most organizations provide formalized training for their employees, but that is not generally a large portion of the training opportunities. Aside from the formal training, which might be in a classroom or online, synchronous or asynchronous, the larger value is tying training to actual performance back on the job. What if a portion of your job responsibilities were tied to helping build other employees' skills in your areas of expertise, and you were rewarded for it? Right now, the way interpersonal skills are transferred occurs within organizations is haphazard, dismissed, and certainly not rewarded or seen as critical to the future success of the organization. Think about all those in the current workforce who will be retiring and all that knowledge that will be lost because we have not developed a good strategy for how to retain it or pass it along to the next generation of workers. This truly is a crisis and certainly something that companies need to address now.

Addressing this issue will require the organization to adopt a means of knowledge management. Categories of job skills will need to be established and kept up-to-date with new skills as they are learned. An organization can use the system to make matches for cross-training between those who have certain skills and those who do not. Tracking needs to be across the organization and not just departments in silos. Thinking about transferable skills and how they might apply to other parts of the organization will be key to challenging the status quo. This is not to be taken lightly and will require work upfront to understand the current knowledge foundation of all employees.

The good news is that you probably already have a lot of the data required for this type of undertaking. Each employee at some point has provided a list of skills, usually in the form of a résumé or CV. Those documents list key words that match the job description that was created by the talent management team, HR, or department leads. Now if an employee has been within an organization for a while, the record of that person's skills may not be up-to-date, especially if the person has moved to other roles.

In this day and age, the average employee stays in a job for about 4.5 years, with younger employees switching more often than older employees. We all know the days of staying with one company or role for decades or a lifetime are pretty much over. The reason I point this out is that the résumé can be used as a tool to establish the baseline of skills and knowledge of workers because it is being updated and refreshed, and therefore is more reliable than HR systems that try to do the same tracking. New technologies, like learning experience platforms, are making this type of data collection and tracking much easier. I have worked with some platforms that can provide reports of what skill sets employees are searching for and what they have noted as expertise. This can be a good starting point in developing an organizational view.

If you want to be truly competitive, consider LinkedIn's new portal called Talent Insights. You can use the information gathered from more than 500 million users across the globe to gain insights into what your competition is doing. For instance, you can run custom reports on a role you are looking to fill. You can filter down the report by location, company, industry, education, and so forth. This data will show you which companies are employing a particular type of talent. Not only that, but you also can see data on each individual company and how many professionals the company employs with a certain skill set, along with growth trends, attrition, and postings of current openings. Imagine the power this will have for competitive intelligence on talent pools and recruiting. This is not a part of the open source of LinkedIn, but a premium package. I think it is worth the investment to stay on top of talent and skills, especially as they are evolving.

Once you have identified all the various skill sets within the organization, you can build a program to start addressing the gaps in skills and knowledge. Employees are used to reaching out and finding information quickly. They need the information at their fingertips. Building networks and groups that facilitate this process will be key in the success of these initiatives. There are many ways employees can share their knowledge with one another if only they knew who needed it. In thinking about how information is shared across social networks, the most impactful and easy to digest information is in the form of videos and pictures. Having employees create these assets on topics in which they have experience can make this learning network come to fruition. You need to make it easy for employees to find what they need. It cannot be buried in file folders, hidden under lock and key, or worse yet, sprinkled over multiple systems or intranet sites within the company. The information needs to be open and transparent in one place that is easily searchable. Think about how you use YouTube for how-to videos on any topic you can imagine. What does that type of asset look like for your organization?

Employees Learning From Others

"Traditionally, the only way the organization developed people was when they moved vertically, but I think now we need to be also much more active in creating mechanisms that allow people to flow and have experiences much more broadly within an organization."

Interview with Kevin Simpson,
Head of Key Account Management Internationally
At a global Pharmaceutical company

The second strategy for developing talent is building a program where employees can learn from others. Some organizations call this a mentorship program. Others call it lunch and learn. Your organization will have to define the right mix of formal versus informal transfer of knowledge. The advantage of having a formal mentorship program is alignment with professional development goals. Based on a specific development plan, mentors and mentees are paired for specific reasons—usually focused on a certain area of the mentor's experience and knowledge. The pairing is critical and must account for personalities and varying values such as culture and perspectives. Many mentorship programs fail because they do not account for these factors, and so the program is dead on arrival. The bottom line is that you cannot roll out a mentoring program without some thought to how the selection process takes place, guidelines for mentor and mentees, and accountability from all involved.

Building networks, either within or outside of organizations, is the best way for employees to keep on top of changes and trends coming to their industries. It will be very important for employees to have strategic connections to those who they can reach out to for advice or knowledge. People are already doing this for everyday decision-making like seeking recommendations for hair stylist to opinions on local schools. Those that are savvy and have a decent network that they trust can pose organizational questions to their network, such as when purchasing a new HR software system or exploring how other industries are incorporating artificial intelligence. These networks are already happening. Are you a part of it? Do you know where to go for advice and knowledge?

My suggestion in looking for the right network is to understand your intent and purpose, and then to search for the right fit. If you are looking outside your organization, you have so many options it can be overwhelming—which is why it is important to think about what you are trying to accomplish before testing out many groups and going down a rabbit hole. There are groups focused on women, industries, technology, hobbies, and more. You name it, you can probably find it, especially online. If you are meeting in person locally, your options may be limited due to the size of your city or town. In any case, to build a solid network, you can't just join a group and expect new connections. You have to show up and get involved. Connections are built over time and generally in a context of projects or services you can provide back to the group. If you join groups online, you can be a lurker, which means just observing. This will not build your network. You need to respond, post, and contribute for others to notice you and build a connection. If you don't, you're just another person on the planet without a personality or face.

Within organizations, it is even more important to step out of your comfort zone and see what is out there. Are there special projects on which you can provide your time or expertise? What about setting up lunch meetings with other leaders in your organization, especially in different functions or departments? By doing so, you can start to build relationships or at least gain insight into their view of the organization? Many organizations have special interest groups or sporting teams; these are also good ways to meet others from different parts of the organization. Getting involved will expand your view and make you a more valuable employee. As a leader, supporting and developing your team outside of traditional feedback on performance and goals is critical. Simply talking about individuals' competencies and behaviors will help raise performance and engagement on your team.

Psychologist Lev Vygotsky developed the concept of the Zone of Proximal Development. In his research, he found that learning happens as we interact with our environment. Developing skills outside of our comfort zone, or as he referred to it as the Zone of Proximal Development, provides opportunities for growth and learning. The trick with this technique in developing others is that the task cannot be too easy or too complex. In either of these extremes, the learner gets complacent or discouraged. It has to be something the learner can almost do but needs some guidance or coaching. The goal of this exercise is that when the task is complete, the learner can do the task on his or her own in the future. The reason it is so tricky is that every employee has different skill sets and experiences, so you as the leader need to be acutely aware of where employees stand before you assign them a task. As a leader, you can also encourage development through group work or collaborative projects with those who already have the skills you want to see developed in your employee.

Personalized Learning

One final strategy for developing talent that I see coming up more often is microlearning and personalized learning paths. I believe this trend will continue and be in demand with the next generations of the workforce. The ways we organize and deliver training programs are going through a major revamp. No longer is the spray and pray approach going to be tolerated or funded. Tying back to knowing who your audience is and what their current capabilities are, developing individualized strategies for employees will be expected. Due to shortage of time and speed of knowledge transfer, organizations will need to redesign their learning strategies to meet the needs of individuals. This will be a complete overhaul for some organizations, but a needed one. By defining what is needed by each employee and when, employees will spend less time on things that don't really matter to them. They will also be able to apply this new knowledge right away in a meaningful manner, which will help with learning transfer and avoid losing critical knowledge. Transparency and clarity are key in defining what employees will need to develop their skills or apply their knowledge. Think of it as just-in-time knowledge or knowledge delivered in bite-sized chunks.

There are new platforms that are making this strategy become a reality and are simplifying the implementation. Speed is key in this new environment we are entering. Generally, these platforms are referred to as Learning Experience Platforms, but they are so new to the market they may have another name by the time you read this. I have recently implemented this type of platform with one of my clients, and I can walk you through one possible way it can be used in your organization. Employees each have their own personalized view and login where they create a profile. During this process, they are asked to pick the skills they are looking to build as well as to identify those they possess already. By the employee selecting key skills, the platform algorithm will know which content, in the form of videos, article, white papers, online courses, and so forth, to serve up to them based on their needs. Every day they can chose to receive lists of recommended content to consume. They can also share and recommend content to others. Depending on your instance, you may be able to tap into employees from other organizations, and you can see what they are consuming. Are you starting to see the power of this type of platform?

Additionally, within a corporate instance of this platform, you can build out your own course offering to include pre-work, links, readings, and participant guides as a truly blended course offering. You can make this course open to all in your organization or to a select group. It is up to you. The biggest feedback I received during the process of implementation is that everyone loved that it was one-stop shopping for learning. They didn't have to hunt around and find information on what is available or where information is housed; it was all in one place. From this system, you can point them to where information is located in your systems or folders. Think about the time savings for each employee—time not wasted searching for things or missing information because they simply didn't know it existed. They also loved that the content was served in 3–5 minute chucks, for the most part (most platforms will give you a time estimate to consume each piece of content), which helps employees manage their time and make the most use of it when they have a moment.

As you can see, many of these strategies reinforce and build on one another. It is important to think of employees' professional development holistically versus one topic at a time. For instance, suppose an employee needs to build project management skills. First, the employee may watch a video to get an overview of what good methods look like. Next, the individual may work with his or her manager to define specific areas to concentrate on to build missing skills or knowledge. Doing so will better define which courses or topic areas to focus on, and they can map out in which format they will achieve their learning and by when. You may want to cap it all off by setting up an employee with a mentor who has proven project management skills and who can oversee and willingly answer questions or concerns as they come up during application of the new skills. This is a more comprehensive plan for talent development that involves multiple layers and departments, all that have a vested interest in making this employee successful so that he or she can be a future leader and develop others. This is a great example of talent enhancement.

Employee Productivity

Lastly, let's talk about employee productivity and what great companies do. A recent study from Bain & Company, a leading consulting firm, found that companies like Apple, Netflix, Google, and Dell™ are 40% more productive than the average company[20]. The way they achieve this is by grouping their top talent on one team on the most important projects or problems within the organization. By doing this, they accelerate strategic initiatives by using the high-potential power. Sports teams do this all the time, so why should companies be any different than other teaming environments? Usually the "A" team members are the best in each position. If the "A" team is better than all the other teams, it is better positioned to be competitive. You concentrate your best players—those with the best record of success—to get you to the final tournament. In business, you are aiming to be the best against your competition. This can be one strategy that will put you above the rest, because most companies tend to spread out their top talent across the organization, which dilutes the value of these employees.

In this type of teaming environment, rewards need to be handled as a group; otherwise the strategy will not work. You want to encourage those top players to work together. It is not about individual glory, but about solving business problems together. Apple uses a collective rewards model that has allowed the company to maintain amazing productivity. Additionally, before diving into any project, the team establishes the rating level at which it will earn incentives, and no one individual can receive a higher rating than the team is given. This is a very different approach than many companies, which generally grade their employees on a scale or distribution method. The latter approach forces HR and business leaders to spread out the talent within designated bands, using a bell curve on which 20% exceed expectations, 60% meet expectations, and 20% do not meet expectations. If you place all of your top talent into one project, you can see how this would be counterintuitive, especially because every team member will expect an "exceed expectations" rating, which is not possible with this distribution system. In fact, it could be seen as a negative to be put on such a project. You can't expect to put your top employees on a project without thinking about all of the correlating factors that tie to their performance and success. The approach needs to be a give and take situation that benefits all parties.

Artificial Intelligence and the Future of Work

You cannot have a conversation about talent without thinking about how technology will impact the future. This means that leaders will need to prepare in order to be successful. We know that our jobs will look different, and we may be eliminating certain tasks within jobs that can be done better by technology— faster and cheaper than we can ever expect humans to perform those tasks. That is reality! So, let's look at ways to prepare ourselves and other leaders for this shift.

To be effective in the coming years, leaders in this new era will need to have key skill sets. We will explore each of these now in detail in the context of leadership within organizations.

Mastering Data Analysis

All leaders will need to master data analysis, because it will be key to driving the business forward. Sure, AI will be taking over some of the tasks, such as crunching the numbers for us; but the real value is interpreting what the data is telling us and figuring out how can we respond or react. There will be an abundance of data that can be sliced and diced many ways, just like statistics. Those who become skillful at deriving insights from the data will ultimately be more competitive.

Being Savvy at Managing Change

If you thought large-scale implementations like Enterprise Resource Planning systems (e.g., SAP®, Oracle®) and Customer Relationship Management systems (i.e. Salesforce® or HubSpot®) were challenging or difficult in the 1990s and 2000s, you will look back and think those were easy compared to what we will experience in the next 10 years. Most research points to failures of these large-scale changes with a whopping 70%+ failure rate sighted by Gallup and other leading consulting firms. This trend will continue if we don't shift our approach to engage employees at all levels in the organization and incorporate them into the evolution of changes.

We are all experiencing change to varying degrees within our organizations. People resist change, especially if they don't understand the thinking behind the change and it seems they are being managed. The challenge is that managers are at the forefront of overseeing the micro-changes happening every day, and it is impossible for a manager to be involved in all of the higher-level conversations. By guiding their teams and engaging in conversations when changes come about, they have a better chance of influencing their employees. You need to realize that employees are trying to make sense of the changes that are already happening. We know there are always multiple change efforts happening concurrently throughout the organization, and this activity will continue. As a leader, you need to understand that the way employees perceive the changes is being discussed all around you within the organization. Employees are interacting within their informal networks within the organization and asking others what they think and how they feel about the changes. These conversations are informal and complex; but if managers spend their time involving themselves in these types of conversations, they will build more influence and positivity to help employees make sense of what is happening versus avoiding these types of conversations and leaving it to chance.

According to research by a leading change management organization, Prosci®, engagement and support of middle managers is one of the keys to success in organizational change efforts. However, the research also found that most middle managers have not received basic training on the skills to lead change and don't understand what is expected of them during this time period. The article titled *Manager/Supervisor's Role In Change Management*[21] suggested that sponsors of the change initiative and change agents should ask three question about this group:

1. Have we told managers and supervisors what we expect from them in times of change?
2. Do they fully understand the specific actions and behaviors we need from them to support a change effort?
3. Have we provided them with the skills and tools to be successful at leading their direct reports through change?

It is critical to provide training on the foundational elements of how people experience change and the associated behaviors so that these leaders can coach their teams through the change. With coaching skills, leaders will be better able to navigate the ups and downs of the change efforts. In many cases, they will be dealing with employees' emotional reactions to the change, which may not seem logical. Organizations need to not just involve these leaders in the changes that are happening to them and their teams, but also to give them the necessary skills and knowledge to be savvy change leaders.

Successful organizations of the future will be so severely disrupted by change that there will be no hiding or halting this process. In fact, if disruption does not occur at all levels in your organization, then that company more likely will not exist in the near future. We have been seeing companies' lifespans on the S&P 500 significantly drop since 1964. A 2018 study from

Innosight® revealed that the 33-year average tenure of companies on the S&P 500 in 1964 had narrowed to 24 years by 2016 and is forecasted to shrink to just 12 years by 2027.[22] The bottom line is that organizations need to evolve and change or they will die.

Improving, Enhancing Targets, Impactful Processes

Leaders will need to understand how technology drives costs out of cumbersome processes. By leveraging Lean and Agile methodologies, leaders can discover the best targets for testing new ideas and streamlining processes. Both of these methodologies focus on driving out waste and making small, incremental changes to work processes. The question will be, "Can AI do it better, faster, and cheaper than a human?" If so, that is probably a good target for implementing a technology solution. Let's not forget the human element in this process. We need to redesign workflows so that there is an understanding of how the new process and roles are enhanced with technology.

To stay competitive, implementation of new technologies will be critical. We are not looking at wholesale replacement of jobs with technology. AI is not advanced enough to replace humans across job sets. According to the authors of *What To Do When Machines Do Everything*[23], look for these characteristics in choosing what tasks to automate:

- **Tasks that are highly repetitive.** Think about high-volume tasks that occur at great scale across your organization.
- **Tasks that need little human judgment.** Think about tasks that have "if-this-then-that" logic and require heavy computation.
- **Tasks that need little empathy.** These tasks are generally not customer facing, although the output is to drive speed and accuracy. These items can include invoicing, scheduling, or claims.

Implementing technology for the right tasks will drive better business results and provide a competitive advantage over other organizations that rely on manual processes.

Making Decisions at the Right Level

Empowering leaders at the appropriate level to make critical business decisions on how to leverage new technology will build agility into the organization. Larger, more established organizations may have a more difficult time letting go of the current power structures. To be competitive in the next 10 years, organizations need to build a start-up mentality, especially in competing with technology hubs like Silicon Valley or Boston.

Leadership and business decision-making will change significantly in the near future. Leaders of established organizations need to shift their mindset from a traditional industrial age structure to a nimble digital structure at all levels of the organization. This will be challenging because there will need to be a balance between localized decision-making and overall strategy of the organization. This will be a tough balance to maintain as this shift is occurring. Each culture will define its unique business models in order to deal with this new reality.

The Talent Progression

I want to encourage you to think about employee development in new ways. I see it as a progression, beginning with focusing our efforts on talent management, such as finding the right person with the right skills to fill a role. The next step is talent development, which is providing skills and experiences for employees to step into new roles, such as a leadership position. Generally, the efforts are targeted at a portion of the employee population and developed for specific reasons, like a new system or process being introduced in the organization. The trainings are usually developed to target specific audiences, but rarely dive down into individual needs. I would like to see organizations get to talent enhancement, where skills and experiences are created at an individual level and each employee has leaders who understand their personal development needs.

I have seen talent enhancement done well by one of my clients. It is more complex than just identifying gaps in knowledge or training employees in new skills. Think of each employee as a hub that has unique needs and experiences. By creating a network of learning, employees can thrive and build meaningful careers. Here are some key components that are needed to enhance employee development:

- Understand what knowledge, skills, and experiences each employee brings to the organization.
- Provide personalized pathways for employees to build upon this foundation of knowledge, skills, and experiences.
- Find ways to grow and expand your employees' viewpoint.
- Pair up employees with senior leaders who can provide different perspectives and exposure to different parts of the organization.
- Understand where your employees want to take their careers.

I worked with a client to leverage new systems that are making these custom employee pathways possible. We thought through the key leadership attributes needed to be successful and then created a flexible environment where employees could access resources for their individual needs and at their own pace. It was a mix of structure and elasticity in one place where they could get information. This particular system also would curate information and provide weekly or daily updates based on the employee's preferences and the skills that employee was trying to enhance. Employees liked the fact that the system was flexible and targeted to them. They also liked the fact that most of the content was no more than 5 minutes long and that each resource included an estimated time to consume. In addition, employees had access to other leaders to help them with the application of new knowledge. Having these leaders available helped drive accountability for incorporating new skills and testing them out. Most employees are able to utilize new knowledge and skills. The bigger question is whether there is support and willingness to incorporate individual growth into the organization. The initiative needs to be supported at all levels; otherwise it is a wasted endeavor.

As you can see, there are major shifts in the way we work and how organizations are structured. How we reward and recognize talent will need to change with this shift. Talent will be much more fluid within organizations, so we need to think creatively about the best ways to leverage our talent pools. Otherwise, they will leave, and the organization will not survive for much longer. Be willing to take some risks. Your employees are counting on it!

Key Takeaways:

✓ Mapping out the landscape of skills within your employees is a good first step toward understanding your organizational capabilities.

✓ Companies have access to new platforms and data sets that allow for easier management of skill sets within and outside of your organization.

✓ Organizations need to provide ways for employees to connect with one another in a meaningful way. This can be through knowledge sharing or mentoring programs and be fostered through an overarching body to provide care and feeding of this network.

✓ Building your network across departments and outside of your place of employment is vitally important to gain new insights and ideas. By leveraging these types of networks, you can solve challenges faster than those without this type of support system.

✓ Use the Zone of Proximal Development model to push your employees to expand their skills and experience. The key is not to assign a task that is either too easy or too difficult because it will discourage development.

✓ Employee development needs to happen at an individual level and be personalized. Also, knowledge should be provided just-in-time, not just-in-case.

✓ Consider putting your top talent in one team for the most critical and strategic value projects. Rewards will need to be aligned at the team level for this approach to work well.

✓ New skill sets for leaders will be needed to navigate and be effective in a technologically changing world.

✓ Being change savvy and understanding the best ways to leverage new technology to enhance the business will make your organization more competitive for the future.

✓ Business models and organizational structures are shifting away from a top-down industrial mentality to an agile digital structure. Leaders need to think what this new structure will look like in their organizations and what needs to happen to make it a reality.

✓ Organizations need to shift from talent management to talent enhancement mindsets. By targeting and personalizing development at the individual level of each employee, leaders can maximize the performance and productivity of their teams.

Leadership

Building Wildly Successful
Global Teams

Let's face it, working across cultures can be challenging. Individuals do not do business the same way everywhere. This is nothing new, and many studies have been focused on the various cultural aspects of our differences. Many of the studies were conducted in the 1950s by researchers such as Geert Hofstede and more recently by Terri Morrison and Wayne A. Conaway, authors of *Kiss, Bow, or Shake Hands.* Morrison and Conaway suggested that people act a certain way if they are from a particular country, but I would argue that it isn't that simple anymore. With the accessibility of social media and globalization, the walls between countries are crumbling. We are exposed to various thoughts from others around the world and are influenced by people we would never have imagined only 10–20 years ago. To be successful in working in today's environment, new skills are needed.

Topics covered in this chapter include:

- The ACE FOCUS model
- Communication and language

The ACE FOCUS Model

I would like to introduce a new model that doesn't even talk about individual countries or regions. The model centers on individual abilities to flex and adapt to other environments. My model is termed ACE FOCUS, which is an acronym for the various key skills I believe you need to be successful in today's global business scenarios.

Adaptability

We will start with the first letter, A for **Adaptability**. It probably doesn't shock you that this is the first part of the puzzle. Those leaders who are not adaptable, from my experience, don't do well in an international setting. You have to be willing to adapt to this new environment. I will give you an example of being adaptable and the benefits.

I will never forget my first experience with cultural shock. I was in Australia for 6 months on a study abroad many years ago. I was one of five students from my university who were chosen for a new exchange program with a university in Australia. When I landed in Sydney, the reality of how far away I was from home hit me. The toilets really do flush in the opposite direction from those in the northern hemisphere. There were strange noises and animals. I ordered a turkey sandwich and it had beets on it, which turned everything purple. The window in my dorm room didn't have a screen on it to block the bugs and birds like the windows at home. In my coursework, I was surprised to learn that there were only one or two exams the whole semester for most of my classes. We also had exams over a 3-week period at the end of the term. I was used to having one week of exams. I have to say it was nice to have them more spread out, so I had more time to study for each one. As you can imagine, there was a lot of content I had to digest and pretty much one shot to get it right, so there was a lot of pressure.

When I first arrived, it was difficult to adjust, and I felt my patience was being tested because things didn't move as fast as I was used to. I hung out with the other American students because it was easier, and they understood my viewpoint. But I realized one day that I was stuck in a fixed mindset and was not be open to the wonderful, new experiences I could have if only I would drop my guard and judgment for a while. This is when living abroad really started to appeal to me, because I was able to appreciate the differences and didn't try to make things the same as what I was accustomed to back home. I opened my eyes to new things, and it served me well. I made lots of new Australian friends, and they even invited me to their homes on breaks. One of my fondest memories was staying with my friend's family in their home in a beautiful location. I could see the ocean right out their window. The family was so warm and open, it felt amazing. My friend's mom actually stated that she was my surrogate mother while I was in Australia. That meant so much to me and made me feel not quite as alone as when I first got there. I take these memories with me everywhere and remind myself when I get frustrated or anxious in my travels to take a step back and take it in. You have to let go of control and go with the flow. In the flow, you can open your mind to new perspectives, and you will never be the same again.

Connection

This leads me to the next letter, C for **Connection**. To work together with other people, you need to find a connection. It helps build trust and it is a human desire to do so. You can connect on many different levels. Perhaps you both have kids. That one is easy, and family is a great way to build rapport across cultures. You could share common activities like running marathons or your love of playing games. Finding something that is truly universal will create a connection and will go a long way to building open communication in order to get things done when it comes to business. There are some cultures that believe in relationships first, so you can imagine it is even more important to find a commonality to build on and move toward mutual goals.

Connecting at a human level with others from around the world can be a challenge. However, in my interview with Mike Williams from Zappos®, he shared a great story of how he builds rapport quickly with others when working across cultures.

> *I often ask myself, how can I create the conditions to go to the next level of understanding in a conversation. To do that I like to ask, "What is your vision for wild success?"*
>
> *Whether I'm talking with a team, individuals, or partners, this question helps reveal what we are all seeing in our mind's eye. I can see what they see from their vantage point. It creates a higher level of shared understanding faster than anything I've ever experienced. It allows us to move towards a vision of wild success that is co-created. All of this builds a more in-depth level of empathy, contextual knowledge, and understanding.*

Empathy

Moving on to the next part of the model, we have **Empathy**. This is a really critical one in leadership in general; but if you don't have empathy for others in other parts of the world, you will have no chance of doing business successfully long-term. To have empathy is to identify the feelings, thoughts, or attitudes of others. It doesn't mean you necessarily agree with them, but more that you understand and can see their perspective.

If you look at any emotional intelligence model, you will find that empathy is one of the most important aspects. When working across cultures, this skill is amplified because, without it, you cannot move forward. There is not a way you can identify with everyone around the world, but it doesn't mean you cannot do business with some people. You have to decide whether the difference is within your value system or how it differs so you don't trip up on areas of disagreement.

I will give you an example from my personal experience. In general, Americans like to move fast in business, and often we are moving so fast that we don't know how something is going to get done or we haven't yet developed a process for it. In working with some of my German clients, this style did not go so well. They have a strong sense of detail and process and want to know exactly how something will be done before moving forward. In fact, we were stuck without that vision or information.

I found this frustrating at first because I was essentially saying, "Trust me, I've been in similar situations and have figured it out." From their perspective, I was being elusive or not trustworthy if I could not tell them how something will be done to exact detail. Once I realized I had an opportunity to be clearer and to outline my process in more detail, I could move forward with the project, and they would support it along the way. I needed to be more detailed so that they knew how we were going to implement the project. Looking back, I appreciate what they were asking for. But when starting our journey, I was frustrated until I changed my mindset and took their perspective and considerations in mind. When I spoke with Mardely Vega, VP of Human Resources for Sodexo® in Latin America, in an interview, she said:

> *When starting in a new company, especially when in a new culture, you need to take the time to absorb, listen, and observe more than you give for the first 3 months. This is what I found to be successful in that transition.*

Now that we have explored ACE, I would like to emphasize that these skills are the foundation to working across cultures. You need to master these before moving on to the next set.

Flexibility

Now we are working on the second part of the model—FOCUS. The F is for **Flexibility**. How is this different than adaptability? When you are being adaptable, you are adjusting yourself in different conditions. I see being flexible as the willingness to yield. You may need to give up something that is important in order to build a relationship or to get a project moving. Flexing is choosing something different than you originally thought. It is a pathway that is being built as you move forward, but it may not be evident what that next steps are. In this instance, you know your options and are developing the way. In contrast, I see adapting as choosing something that wasn't on the table before, but was revealed later on. I will demonstrate flexibility in an international setting in my next story.

My first really foreign experience for work was traveling to China. I was asked to work with my sales colleague and our local instructor in China to help secure a new client. We were given a week to explore and gather training requirements for the company. That was quite a long time; normally we are only given a day, if that. So, I was not really sure what to expect. I traveled to Shanghai and then to Shenzhen. This was a high-tech company that built a large campus for its employees. It was quite impressive. We started our first day with introductory presentations and got to understand who would be on our team. This took us until lunch, so we were then taken to the cafeteria that was on campus as well. It was nice to get to know our hosts better, and we found out some more personal things. They were impressed that I knew how to use chopsticks.

After we finished lunch, we were asked whether we needed a rest. In the United States, you would *never* be asked that question, so I wasn't quite sure how to answer. I took the lead from my sales manager who headed up the China office. He was also thrown by the question (he is European), but he insisted we continue with the meeting. Our hosts were a little thrown off by our response, and it led to an interesting turn of events. We were escorted back to the conference room and, as we were walking through the office, all the lights were off. Employees had their heads on the table. Later I noticed that some employees had cots at their desks as well. The lights were out in *all* of the offices. I have never seen such a thing and started feeling like I was intruding. Once we got to the conference room, our host knocked on the door and a very sleepy-looking employee greeted us. Apparently, employees used the conference room as a place to sleep as well, so they were not happy we were disturbing their routine. At this point, we realized we were not going to make any progress, and our hosts were looking tired. We resigned to the fact that we would be taking a break for about an hour, so we decided to sit in the café while they had their rest. This is the end of part 1 of the story. I will pick up this story after the next skill is introduced.

Openness

The story leads nicely to our next part of the model, O for **Openness**. For all of this to work, you need to be open to the possibilities. Having a fixed or closed mindset will not bode well for you in working globally. You have to be open to new ideas, things, ways of doing, and so forth. Being open really drives diversity of thought if you are not limiting yourself to one way. Think of it as opening the door to a world you haven't seen before. It is not for the faint of heart, but if you are willing to grow and learn, you may be surprised at what you learn or can leverage in the future.

Picking up the previous story from my China experience, my colleagues and I got to the café and we were in disbelief of the events that just happened. We had never encountered this type of behavior within a large corporate entity. All the employees took a rest from 1:00 to 2:00 in the afternoon, and this was the daily routine as we would soon find out. Luckily, we had our Chinese instructor who explained the reasoning to us. In Chinese culture, it is common for those employees who work very hard and long days to take a rest in the middle of the day after lunch. I guess now that I think about it, it isn't that different from a siesta. The only difference is that employees go home for a siesta, whereas in this Chinese company they rested in the workplace. An afternoon rest is supposed to boost productivity, and I can certainly see the possibilities. I am not sure whether our hosts were more productive in the afternoon with having a rest, but it seems to work for them.

It took a little getting used to, but by the end of the week we had our routine down. As our hosts would go for their rest after lunch, we would hang out in the café for an hour. It gave us some time to strategize and assess how the days were going, so I guess in the end it wasn't all that bad. I will never forget the image of sleeping employees with their heads down, lights out, cots pulled out from under desks. I am sure our hosts thought we were strange for not taking a rest, but I don't think I could take a rest at work. It just seems counterintuitive to me, but that is because Americans work for 12 hours straight on a regular basis. We think that it is normal, and our bosses expect that of us. I must say that it would be highly frowned upon to find an employee sleeping, maybe even cause for dismissal, so our perspectives are very far apart. I know that a very few progressive companies in the United States have resting areas, but it is a very new concept for us. I am not sure whether it will ever catch on in U.S. corporations, but wouldn't it be nice to have a breather in the middle of a stressful day? I have to say, I think the Chinese have this one right.

Collaboration

We are now working so well, we can move to our next part, which is C for **Collaboration**. You can see why I put this skill here. If you don't have the previous parts, then collaboration is just not possible. It means working in concert like an orchestra. You understand how others do things and they understand you. The feeling is mutual, and you are getting things done no one thought possible. It is a really good spot to be in when you are in this stage. Everyone on the team is contributing and feeling good about the direction. There is established trust and respect with one another. You are moving things forward, and it doesn't feel like hard work.

I am big fan of working across time zones. I have worked and continue to work in teams where the tasks are divided up and are complimentary to each other. To give you an example of how this works, I will set a task during my workday and hand it to my team in another time zone usually through an email exchange. They will pick up the email when they arrive at work [sometimes there is an overlap between myself and the team lead in the other time zone which I find as a best practice to clarify any questions or challenges to getting the task done]. That team will work on the task during their workday and when I arrive back in the office the next day I either have an update on the status or confirmation of the completion of the task. Having the extension of my team in various areas around the world allows the company to be much more productive as long as there is a high level of collaboration.

One way to bridge the gap to collaboration is to bring people together. Not all companies or organizations can do this, but it is highly effective. The act of meeting people in person builds a bond and allows you to put a face with a name. You get to know them as individuals and, hopefully, more about them beyond work. I see this approach work well as an annual strategic planning meeting or summit for the top executives of a company. By allowing them to participate in the vision or goals for the coming year (or 3 years, if you dare), you build understanding and buy-in at a deeper level within that team. Many employees take cues from their highest level of leader in the organization. So, by building this understanding across the key departments, you can start to collaborate in a more meaningful way to support the common goals. I also find this true in a project or consulting environment when people are spread across various regions. The projects I was involved in that kicked off with a face-to-face meeting were much more successful than those in which I didn't have the opportunity to meet the people on the team I'd be working with. It is difficult to be angry or have misunderstandings with those whom you have met than those you haven't.

Understanding

This leads me to introduce our next part of the model, U for **Understanding**. You need to do your research on not only the culture of the country, but also ways of doing business in general. I remember a specific event that happened while I was working in Europe. Many of the countries in Europe greet one another by kissing on the cheeks. If this is not awkward enough for an American, add the fact that depending on which country or even region will determine the number of air kisses. One of my wise U.S. colleagues who lived in London gave me this advice: Air kisses always start on the left side, and just go with the flow for how many based on who you are interacting with. I thought this was great advice and for the most part it was true, until it wasn't. For some reason, a client started the air kiss on the right side, which completely through me off. I got so embarrassed and I am sure turned a bright red. However, in that moment, I remembered the other piece of advice my colleague told me. He said it is okay to admit that you are not familiar with this custom and are open to learning. I used this moment to do exactly that, turning the situation into a learning moment and apologizing to my client. The client was very understanding and didn't seem to take offense. I have to say, after that incident I was cautious on which side to start the air kisses.

When studying and preparing for work with people from different parts of the world, it is important to think about culture in three parts, as described in my interview with Marcus Simmonds, CEO of Tortuga® Rum Cakes:

> *There are different types of cultures. You have people who have their own personal culture. The business has a culture. The country which you*

operate has another culture. Getting all three of those in some level of commonality and equilibrium can be extremely challenging. We strive for the company to be on organization across the board, you want it to be a multinational entity but with one set of values, regardless of everyone operating in different environments with different needs and wants. For example, every country has different holidays so which ones does the organization recognize? Does the U. S. company recognize the Jamaican holidays, or the Jamaican company recognize the Cayman Islands holidays? Which ones do you recognize for your business to run without disruption? You have to manage those sorts of idiosyncrasies to be successful.

Self-Awareness

I will wrap up with the last essential element of a global leader: S for **Self-Awareness**. This is where emotional intelligence skills come in handy. Being in touch with how you are reacting and interacting with others from around the world is so important. You will find yourself in new situations and sometimes be the only one who does not speak a certain language. That is okay. You cannot possibly learn all the languages around the world. Be cognizant, though, of how you are waiting for others' conversations to end. Sometimes it is necessary to have your host or colleague make another person feel welcome before jumping into a common language, which is typically English in business settings. Most of my business meetings do not have interpreters, and you won't always have that luxury.

When people are speaking a language you don't understand, here's a tip for conducting yourself while this is occurring. I always listen with interest to see whether I can decipher any of the words being spoken. It is a kind of game I play to keep my interest and pay attention. I have managed to pick up some foreign words here and there along the way. In these situations, we need to pay attention to our thoughts, reactions, and emotions. Pay special attention to your nonverbal cues, because they will give away the uncomfortable feelings you may be experiencing in the moment. Just accept that it is normal to feel this way, and the feeling will soon pass. We are building new neural pathways in our brains, which is good and keeps us stimulated as humans.

In this next insight from my interview with Kevin Simpson, Head of Key Account Management Internationally at a global Pharmaceuticals company. He is a very wise global leader who shares his thoughts on being more self-aware and mindful with our colleagues around the world:

> *I am constantly stunned by the lack of [cultural awareness] of those whose native language is English (like people from the United States or the United Kingdom) when they speak and communicate in ways that just are not understandable to multiple people across the world. [There is a tendency to] use jargon, acronyms, and business speak that has no way of translating to others who aren't from that culture. It is not the accent or jargon, per se, but the lack of consideration to actually communicate with others that don't have the same background or culture as you. Take time to stand in their shoes and see how things look from their perspective every so often.*

If you hone your skills in these areas, you will be well on your way to becoming a successful global leader. Just realize that it is a journey, so you will always be tested and put into new situations. I don't want to completely discount the value of knowing nuances of various cultures. Also, please do not assume that if another country's language is the same language as yours that they are the same. Probably not! As they say about England and America, they are two nations separated by a common language. Language is one area, but it is important to tune up your cultural intelligence as well. If there are norms or taboos, you certainly don't want to misstep if you can avoid it. Just knowing some basic things will help, and I suggest doing a little research before heading to or working with those from other countries. YouTube is a great way to research behavioral norms of how various cultures from around the world define these norms. Just realize with today's connected world and individual personalities, values and norms in different cultures are measured on a sliding scale depending on an individual's experience and/or willingness to be exposed to different ways of thinking and working. One size does not fit all within a culture or country.

Becoming a successful global leader require us to be continually learning and exploring. Being open-minded is a key way to build rapport across cultures. When you communicate with those from other cultures, use the opportunity to test your listening and observing skills. Slow down, especially your spoken word, to communicate at a deeper level. Pull in your colleagues on virtual meetings to be sure all voices are heard. As a leader, you want to be inclusive and find ways for others to jump in and allow space for all to participate in a way that makes everyone feel comfortable. This might take some trial and error, but you will find what works for you and your team.

I also want to point out logistics in working with others from around the world. We know that if we are working with colleagues from the other side of the world, we will never find a mutual time that will be within normal business hours for everyone. So, be cognizant of the times you're scheduling these meetings. Don't always schedule meeting times that are convenient for your own time zone. Take turns meeting outside of normal business hours. Another logistical factor can be Internet connectivity, which is not the same around the world. I do prefer to have meetings where participants can see others by using video functionality, but the bandwidth does not always allow for that, especially if you have a large group on the line. I would certainly try as much as possible to utilize video when meeting virtually. Seeing a face is better than just hearing a voice. Here is what Don

Stanley, an Enterprise Learning and Leadership Development leader at Grainger®, said in my interview with him:

To be an effective global leader is really to be inclusive and make sure that you're not just forcing what is convenient for you.

Communication and Language

A behavior that throws off many Westerners is when other cultures say "yes," but they don't really mean it. The reason for this is a phenomenon known as *saving face*. Now, this isn't just on one side. The gesture is meant for both parties, because they don't want to make you feel awkward when they cannot deliver, and the word "no" just isn't in their vocabulary. Try to step in their shoes and understand while asking yourself, "Am I requesting an impossible deliverable or task in this timeline?" They want to honor the relationship and avoid humiliation or embarrassment, and they believe sometimes it is better to let someone be wrong than to point out that the person is wrong.

Another clue is giggling or a nervous laugh, which can indicate that someone is not comfortable with the conversation. Pay attention to these reactions because you are probably risking *loss of face,* which is the opposite of *saving face.* The way to overcome this, if you start noticing deliverables are being delayed or tasks not being done, is to use that opportunity to ask exploratory questions. Don't blame; instead, come from a place of openness and understanding. You could ask, "This didn't work as we expected; what could we try now?" The context of the exploration is important as well. Many times, asking in front of a group is not the correct way to approach this situation. You can have smaller group or individual conversations that will make all parties more comfortable in being honest. For some cultures, it is not good to point out someone's mistakes openly in front of their peers. Start to pay attention to the language being used. If you hear, "We will get back to you" or "We will do our best," you can assume that means "no." Lastly, be willing to negotiate and look for ways that everyone involved feels respected.

When I had the opportunity to work with mostly European and Asian companies, my perspective changed on how to be an effective global leader in different cultural contexts. I was more aware of the signals I gave off without even realizing it. For instance, there is sensitivity in certain parts of the world to American English versus UK English. Now you might think, well, at the end of the day it is still English; but watch out for the subtle differences, such as certain spellings, for instance, *color* versus *colour* or *tire* versus *tyre*. Imagine how confusing this can be for nonnative English speakers who are trying to interpret written communications. Even the way I started phrasing my communications became much more in line with a European mindset. It is funny, but I didn't even notice this was happening until my sister pointed out to me one day that my emails were very British sounding. At first, I didn't know what she was talking about, but after she pointed it out, I began to understand what she meant. It was just a little shift in my tone and vocabulary, and probably some spelling too, as I adopted the British ways of communicating.

Effective communication is not just in what we say, but even in how we say it, or even in how we don't say anything at all. You may have heard about anthropologist Edward T. Hall's research on low-context and high-context cultures. If you do a lot of work with Asian teams or clients, this is a really important behavior to understand. In low-context cultures, communications are fairly straightforward and to the point. Pretty much, you say what you mean, and you mean what you say. As you can imagine, many of the low-context cultures are in the west. Now, in high-context cultures, communications are much more nuanced and not straightforward. There are messages between the spoken words that are rooted in the culture. Very often the messages are implied and not fully explained. You are just supposed to figure it out from the context. You can imagine for a western mindset that this can be quite difficult from a couple of perspectives. One, you have to shift your mindset to receive indirect communication. In addition, you have a disadvantage because you lack the cultural context of the message that is perfectly clear to others in the culture. Some examples of high-context cultures are Japan, Indonesia, and many Arab countries.

When I first started working with a Swedish office, I felt we had some misinterpreted communications. My colleagues' emails were very short, and I felt like I was coming into the conversation late because I was missing information. I was perplexed about why they weren't giving me all the information I needed to complete the task. So, I asked my other colleague, who is also Swedish but based in the same office as I am, for some help in deciphering the communications. I was a little surprised by her answer, but it made complete sense once she explained it to me. The reason for the behavior was that they didn't want to burden me by asking for something directly; they wanted to avoid any possibility for conflict. The challenge I had with this style was that we were not in the same physical office, so I didn't have any background information or context for the work. That made it impossible for me to fulfill their requests. What I found worked best was to build the relationships with those team members so that they felt comfortable when I reached out for more information. I tried to talk to them on the phone, if possible, when I needed background information for making a decision on how to fulfill their request. It took a little getting used to, but after some practice and rapport-building, it started getting better.

A last piece of advice is to be sure that your communications do not include references to sports or local sports teams. For instance, I have often seen and heard references to American football or baseball, which as you can imagine don't translate to contexts outside of the United States. Imagine if someone used a cricket reference in the United States. There aren't many American cricket fans or people knowledgeable about that sport, so the point would be lost. Our businesses are filled with business jargon and acronyms. When working in global teams, avoid them as much as possible. An example is the business expression "Think outside the box." A literal translation for a nonnative English speaker might be misinterpreted. To be fair, Americans are not the only ones guilty of using language that doesn't translate well, but I do see many examples of this behavior in my work with multicultural teams. All I ask is for you to be more aware of your communication and try to mitigate misunderstandings as much as possible. At the end of the day, our goal is to be better global leaders and to work better together. As a leader, it is your responsibility to make sure all of your team members, regardless of where they sit in the world, are happy and productive employees who feel included in ways that makes them feel good.

Good luck in reaching the summit in your global journey!

Key Takeaways:

✓ Using the ACE FOCUS model, you can hone your success in working with teams globally.

✓ **Adaptability** means being open to new perspectives.

✓ **Connection** is even more important if you are virtual or not in the same location. By looking for ways to build the connection, you can go to higher levels of understanding, including the context of culture and language.

✓ To have **Empathy** is to identify the feelings, thoughts, or attitudes of another. It doesn't mean you necessarily agree, but that you understand and can see their perspective.

✓ **Flexibility** in a global team setting is to give up something in order to build on the relationship or push the project forward.

✓ In the model, O is for **Openness**. You need to be open to the possibilities of new ideas, thoughts, and ways of doing things.

✓ By building off the previous global attributes, **Collaboration** is when the team is acting like a well-oiled machine. Trust and respect have been established, and goals are being met without much extra effort.

✓ **Understanding** is doing research on how business is done in any environment you are working in outside of your own. You don't need to be an expert, but at least attempt to embrace a different way in order to communicate effectively.

✓ Lastly, **Self-Awareness** in a global setting is knowing yourself in unfamiliar settings. We all feel awkward when we don't know the language or customs. By being aware of your unconscious reactions, you can learn from the situation even if you don't know what the others are saying.

✓ Considering the rules of conduct when working together is important to respect your team. Be cognizant of time zones and try to meet using video so you can have a face and voice to build understanding.

✓ Communications and language are where most teams find a disconnect. Especially when working with those where English is not their native language, be careful of the context of messages and minimize the use of sports analogies and business jargon. These just don't translate well.

Overcoming Your Biggest
Leadership Challenges

We are living in a world that is changing fast and getting more complex. In this environment, leadership is difficult—no one ever said or thought it is easy. People are an organization's greatest asset, many say, but it is not followed up with action, and employees are disappointed at the lack of caring, development, or career paths. This is a business risk and needs to be addressed along with a much larger focus. The talent in our organization is key to our success in the workplace. If our best talent is going out the door, we will have shortages of critical roles, and our leadership pipelines will be scarce in the future. How do you know where to focus your efforts to be the most effective leader? Let's go into more detail now on how to challenge yourself in new ways to meet this demand.

Topics covered in this chapter include:

- Firefighting
- Motivation
- Focus
- Productivity
- Vulnerability
- Failure
- Perfectionism

Firefighting

The first thing you need to do is stop firefighting. What do I mean by that? You get distracted and pulled into the immediate needs or tasks in front of you. The question is, does reacting in this way bring the most long-term value for you, your team, and the organization? It is easy to jump into a tactical problem because it feels good to find resolution and it gives you a sense of accomplishment. I challenge you to step back and evaluate the situation before jumping feet first into these types of situations. Sure, you will have problems arise that you have to tackle right away, but I would say 70% of these situations are not critical and do not need your attention right in that moment. By allowing ourselves to focus our efforts on the constant demands for your attention, we are distracted from the more important goal of building our teams.

Obviously, you cannot spend all of your time in developing your team. That is not realistic. However, I would highly recommend you spend at least 20% of your time coaching and mentoring others for their benefit and the benefit of your organization. Schedule this time like you would any other meeting. Plan for these conversations and understand that you are guiding and not telling them how to be better. You will need to ask powerful questions to get your team members involved with their own development and to own the outcomes. Where you are guiding them will determine the types of questions you will ask. It is better to ask open-ended questions (i.e., ones that cannot be answered with "yes" or "no") so you can gain perspective about how they think and approach challenges, understand where they are coming from, and begin to understand their perspective. Here are some questions to get you started:

- If you could do it over again, what would you do differently?
- What is the opportunity here?
- What is the challenge?
- What is the part that is not yet clear?

- How do you want it to be?

I will give you an example of when I was caught in firefighting mode, and it hurt me professionally. I stepped up to a director role in another country, where I was asked to build the capacity of my newly formed department in this region. As you can imagine, it was a daunting task, but I was up for the challenge. I fully expected to build this amazing team and have time to develop and coach them. Unfortunately, I quickly jumped into the multitude of actions and tasks that needed my attention, which did not include developing my team. Our region was so successful in acquiring new clients, and much of the time-consuming work fell on my team to deliver on what was sold. It was a tall order, and my team and I were having trouble keeping up. Not only that, but we also had critical department handoffs that were not well established and not ready to handle the volume of work coming through.

We wanted to drive sales and revenue, especially through new clients. But because we never set the foundation for how to get things done between departments—that is, who was responsible, what the tradeoffs and guardrails were—we struggled to handle the current capacity of work. The processes and workflow were haphazard and not well understood. I was so busy trying to keep up with our client demand that I really had no time, or so I thought, to develop my team. Once we finished one project, the next one was lined up to start. There was no room to breathe, step back, and evaluate what was working and what was not, and we had a lot that was not working. I felt exhausted and constantly stressed. I never had the sense of accomplishment because it was always more, more, more! I felt it taking a toll on my health and, to be frank, I thought I could easily suffer a heart attack or stroke at any moment. This is not a good place to be as a leader. Does any of this resonate with you?

I was always the first one in the office and the last one to leave. I even got locked into my office in London once. The security guard bolted the door on his way out at 8 p.m., so I couldn't get out of the office until the morning. This was truly a low point for me, being locked in my office overnight, but it gave me time to rethink what I was doing and how much time I was spending on trivial tasks.

The big question to ask yourself is whether you would like to be seen as a leader or a manager. What is the difference? Generally speaking, a leader uses influence and inspires teams to get things done. People follow leaders. A manager tends to be more directive, as in a command and control style, telling employees what to do. People work for the manager, but this role is viewed as controlling an outcome. From this perspective, managers can get stuck by managing tasks that are right in front of them rather than delegating them. They can feel as if they will never get out from behind the huge pile of demands and tasks requiring their attention outside of their team. Does this sound like an inspirational leader that you would want to work for? I am thinking not, and this is why you need to be aware that if you get stuck in this cycle, it will suck all the life out of you and eventually your team.

I finally realized the toll my firefighting was taking on my team and made a choice to stop focusing on what was right in front of me or who was shouting the loudest. To take back control, I needed a strategy that helped regain my sanity and gave me ownership. What did I do? I actually started working less and scheduled focused times for all of my key responsibilities. This allowed me to bring balance back into my life.

From that point on, I decided to arrive at the office at the normal start of the day. I made sure to incorporate a break in the middle of the day, even if it was just a 15-minute walk around the block outside. It was important to get away from my desk and computer to get fresh air. Surprisingly, the break boosted my productivity, I was much more efficient in my tasks in the afternoon, and I could leave at a decent hour. I was no longer the last one to leave the office every night. I also made efforts to spend more development time with my direct reports. In doing that, I realized I could delegate more and give some developmental opportunities to those on my team. It felt great to lift some of the burden off my plate and also to see my team grow their skills. It was a win-win situation.

> *"No one saves us but ourselves. No one can and no one may. We ourselves must walk the path."*
> Buddha

By shifting my viewpoint about my team, I was able to think about them as future leaders within the organization. I was giving them opportunities to show their strengths and was building up their experience and confidence.

Motivation

Another challenge I see with leaders I work with has to do with motivation. Have you ever experienced a time when you were on a high-performing team? There have been particular moments in my career that I remember in the moment thinking, "Wow! That was an amazing experience and I want to learn as much as possible from this situation." When I reflect back on these moments, I think about what made everything work so well. I experienced strong leaders who respected all that we had to offer, and they leveraged our strengths. We also had unified goals and personal goals we were working toward. Everyone in that department, at all levels, was learning from one another, because we knew we all had different life and career experiences to share that were valuable.

Why is it so difficult to achieve this kind of zen-like team? What are some obstacles in achieving high-performing teams? There are many things that get in the way—from your personal style, to the reporting structure of the organization, and to the culture of the team. We have all experienced, in ourselves or in other leaders, challenging situations like denying there is a problem or deferring responsibility.

In driving for higher-performing teams, we need to shift our mindset to overcome these challenges and focus our efforts for better outcomes. I have seen leaders with positive outlooks have better outcomes than those who are negative. The way we perceive our work and our disposition have a huge influence on how our team feels about the work. It is absolutely imperative to create an environment where employees feel good about their sense of accomplishments.

Focus

As a leader, where you focus your time and energy has a direct impact on how successful you will be as a leader in your approach to the work environment. You have a choice about how you interact with others. If you look at certain situations from a macro-level, like overall organizational culture or your discouragement working with your direct leader, it doesn't give you a way to empower yourself to take control over the situation. However, if you think about ways you can directly impact or change situations that are challenging, then you might realize the change you seek because you have more influence over it. For instance, you could choose to be a better role model or build out your network within the organization. Essentially, what you focus your attention on directly impacts your effectiveness across work and even beyond, including family, health, finances, and more.

The challenge with focusing our time and efforts in the overarching space of our organizations is that many things are out of our control and we have limited influence, especially in large organizations. If we, as leaders, stay at this level, then we could be wasting a lot of effort and start to feel frustrated that nothing is changing. Essentially, at the end of the day, it is too big of a challenge to tackle easily, so we waste time spinning our wheels thinking about what could be. We spend our energies on "if only" scenarios instead of breaking down the issues into more manageable chunks that can have an impact.

To have more impact, we need to bring our thoughts and actions down to a more localized level. Instead of playing a victim role and being reactive, you can shift to being proactive and action oriented. Think about your goals and the challenges you have in obtaining those within your organization (or beyond). Really examine what is holding you back. Are there things that you can do and have influence over to change the path or outcome? The way you approach a situation can really change the outlook and outcome.

Let's look at two opposing perspectives to demonstrate what I mean. What if you feel your workload is too heavy? If you frame your thoughts from this view, then you can feel overwhelmed and not empowered to do anything about it. What can you do to turn this thought around? How about working to clarify with your manager your areas of focus that align with the business priorities? This allows you to be in control of the situation and have meaningful conversations with your leadership about where to focus your efforts for the most impact. In contrast, framing your thoughts from a defeatist view where you believe you can't rectify the situation leaves you without focus and direction. My advice to be a more effective leader is to approach challenges with an eye for action, even if you can impact only a couple of items. At least you can start from there and see how it goes. Focusing on the things you can do something about allows you to be more in control. You have a choice about how you spend your time and effort. My advice to you: Choose wisely!

This action-oriented perspective takes practice and conscious effort. I recommend working with a coach or your manager on what you should be focused on at work to gain clarity and to align yourself with the organizational goals. In the same way, you can do this with your team so they can learn to be more proactive and focused. We can't be involved in everything. Learn how to guide your team to apply their valuable resources to the areas with the greatest potential impact.

Productivity

Another challenge we have with our teams is the disappearance of a standard work day. We live and work in a 24/7 world. News used to be once, maybe twice per day, but now it is instantaneous. Same thing with our organizations—what we are being asked to do isn't contained nicely in a 9 to 5 job anymore. How do we help our teams to find a balance, so they are not working 12+ hours per day?

You need to focus on productivity. Why? Because we have limited energy and time to invest in any given task. By demonstrating healthy behaviors like eating right, getting enough sleep, and spending time outside of work, we encourage the same in our teams. Having healthy habits, being able to manage emotions, and applying focused attention on tasks are closely correlated. Work with your team to determine the best way to use their energy levels and encourage them to listen to their bodies when they need a break, either mental or physical.

You can also provide guidelines on what you expect from your team. For instance, I would let my team know that when I was on the road traveling and there was an urgent need to speak to me, they could text me and I would get back to them the first chance I had. This guideline allowed them not to expect an immediate response, but to know that I would respect the urgency of needing to discuss a situation. There are many things you can do with your team to encourage boundaries in the workplace as well as to provide more flexibility if the task requires time outside of normal business hours. Find ways to give employees back some of their time—so they don't feel the organization is always taking every waking minute—should be a priority for finding a balance and supporting longevity.

Vulnerability

To be an effective leader, I encourage you to show vulnerability. This trait is truly one of the most difficult parts of being a leader. One of the leading researchers and TEDx top speakers, Brené Brown described vulnerability like this: "Lean into the discomfort. You have to give opportunities to show your true self to others. Have the courage to be imperfect and to tap into your authentic self. This is essential for connection." Her TEDx event on YouTube[24] currently has more than 37 million views. If you haven't seen it, you should check it out.

In her research, Dr. Brown found a surprising fact about those who embraced vulnerability. She discovered that those who were honest with themselves and accepted the imperfect parts of themselves had more compassion toward others. By letting go of control, you can look past the failings of others and appreciate their efforts. Let in the experience and don't let yourself go numb, but rather look toward how it allows you to grow as a person or employee. Dr. Brown suggested that people (leaders) who embraced vulnerability were viewed more favorably than leaders who did not. Employees want leaders to show that they are not perfect. Employees don't want uncaring robots as their managers.

Part of what Dr. Brown's research showed was the need for authenticity, flexibility, and a desire for connection. We will explore each of these aspects now in the context of what it means as a leader.

Authenticity, **flexibility**, and **connection**. These are the three words I hear consistently from leaders when they discuss how to achieve synergy within a team.

Authenticity

Let's explore how to be an authentic leader and the importance to your team. Have you experienced leaders who weren't bringing their true selves to work? Did you feel they were hiding from something or acting in a way other's expected them to? We all have met leaders that we sensed weren't quite trustworthy. Employees, and especially those on your team, will pick up on the need you feel to "put on an act" at work in a leadership role. You may think you are doing a good job at being what you think you should be or emulating someone else's style, but your team is good at picking up signals that you are not being your true self.

When you show your honesty, your team will build the trust and respect you are hoping to achieve. This behavior also ties closely to building an ethical foundation as a leader. Doing so allows the team to be open with you because the trust goes both ways. It can build a positive work environment because the team members do not feel they will be thrown under the bus at any moment. How many of us have experienced the finger pointing in our direction for something that went wrong and have alone shouldered the blame for it? Many employees have stood alone in these situations, which is unfortunate.

How do you create an authentic and positive environment for your team? The first element ties back to being emotionally intelligent especially from a self-awareness perspective. You have to know how you are being perceived by others in the things that you do and say. By knowing yourself, you can recognize when you are deviating from your true, authentic self. You also need to be genuine to yourself and others. Transparency is key to this element. Your team will quickly pick up on nonverbal signals, especially if they are incongruent with other aspects of your leadership or work.

Another piece of authenticity is having a balanced perspective. We all have unconscious biases, and they play out in our working with others. In recognizing these areas of bias, realize that you may have blind spots. You can mitigate those areas or at least recognize when you are being unfair in a situation so that you can get better at combating those behaviors. Being fair to all does not always mean being equal. It means you give all people a chance to excel wherever they might be in their career path or trajectory.

Lastly, authenticity means that when it comes down to it, you will do the right thing. One of the most universal ethical beliefs, regardless of culture or religion, is the moral imperative to treat others as you want to be treated. Be sure to be empathetic to your team's concerns and the journey they are on. Organizations can feel like a rollercoaster ride sometimes, and I am afraid this will only get worse in the coming years. If you are a leader of integrity, your team will ride the wave with you, even though they may need to hold on with everything they've got. But with the trust you have built and the respect you have earned, they will believe you will be forthright and honest with them even if that means you have to say, "I don't know, but when I do, I will let you all know."

At the end of the day, your team will determine whether you are an authentic leader or not. It is one of those intangible qualities that most people can intuitively sense. It is not something you can fake, so don't try. This is the difficulty with being an authentic leader, because each leader will be different. But that is the point. Teams don't want cookie-cutter leadership; they want you to be yourself but also have the team's best interest at heart with everything you do.

You might be asking how to demonstrate authenticity to your team. It ties back to really knowing yourself and your values. We each have our unique style and preferences. For instance, some of us are more extroverted than introverted in our preference of how we gain energy. We may have certain political beliefs that guide our community values. We could follow various religious beliefs. All of these things factor into our true selves and how we show up at work. Employees should understand that others we work with may not have the same energy, political, or religious grounding as you do, and that is okay. Be vigilant not to use your judgment of these factors on others. Instead, balance demonstrating your belief system with open respect for others who may feel differently. Approach others with curiosity and open-mindedness, and respect their perspective. That will go a long way toward building and deepening trust and authenticity.

Connection

This element is one of the easiest to do, but the most often neglected. Once you become a leader, it is your responsibility to understand your team from many aspects. Looking at individuals on the team as unique and understanding what motivates them is extremely important. This can go beyond work and certainly is a must in global teams. I have seen very successful and respected leaders who know every person they come in contact with during their workday. It is as simple as knowing the café workers' names. Do they have children? In your global teams, what foods do they enjoy? Are they the same favorites as yours?

For your team to believe you care, you have to show it. We spend so many hours of our days at work. Sometimes we see our coworkers more than our families. Be sure to embrace those moments that a connection is revealed. It is something as humans we all aspire to have.

In my interview with Garry Ridge, the CEO of WD-40® Company, he described the culture at his company, which we all can take a lesson from:

> *People are still people. They want to be treated with respect and dignity. Most of us want to learn something new every day. We want to have the freedom to be able to be involved, and the reason people want to be involved is they want to feel like they've made a contribution. One of our biggest human desires we have is to belong.*

We are all human. We have hobbies, and most of us have a family. It is finding those things we have in common that we can talk about regardless of where we are in the world. The best dispersed projects I have been on were the ones that kicked off with an initial face-to-face meeting. It is difficult to be mad at someone you have met in person and understand as a human being.

One secret shared in an interview with Cathy Susie, VP of Human Resources for Schneider Electric™, is to put a picture of whomever you have a virtual meeting with on your computer screen or have it next to you to help make that connection, as if they are right next to you. Otherwise, it is too easy to multitask or get distracted by something else. You need to give the person your undivided attention, as if that person were face-to-face. In addition, her team uses a WhatsApp® group to tell funny stories, share vacation pictures, and congratulate one another (e.g., birthdays, weddings, recognition). That is how team members connect with one another regularly on a personal level.

Flexibility

The other trait mentioned consistently by inspirational leaders was giving the space for your team members the flexibility to grow and try new things. This means that they will make mistakes, and they sometime will fail. But encourage them to take on new challenges, because that is how you and the team will learn the most. You can build an environment where employees feel they can learn and grow and not feel fearful that any minute they might get fired for failing after trying something new.

In order for our employees to grow, they will need the flexibility to take some risks which means they might not get it right every time. Many of us, as leaders, hate the word *failure* because the word holds a strong negative connotation. The interesting thing is that we all need to learn from things that we do—in the form of experiences or just plain trial-and-error.

Things just don't go well all the time. That is reality! What if we reframed our perception of failure to mean learning lessons? By shifting our mindset to approach a situation as more exploratory versus accusatory, we switch to a coaching role. By allowing your employees to determine *how* they will approach tasks versus telling them *what* they should do, you can observe their thought processes and approaches, which can give you better insight on best ways to coach them through challenges. In many situations, you'll never have all the information to make a decision to move forward, so you and your team have to be okay with taking some risks. Just be sure they are educated risks. Therein lies the challenge.

Here are some questions you can ask during this exploratory conversation:

- How do you think this situation/task went?
- What did you do and what was the result?
- What, if anything, would you do differently next time?

By asking these three simple questions, you can have a meaningful conversation and get further insight into that person's actions versus beating that person down because something didn't go as planned. Be cognizant of the words you use and really try to stay away from negative words. You need to practice the delivery of the message and chose your words carefully, because the conversation can have very different outcomes if not handled right. Addressing failure is a skill. In coaching models, you will find there are times to be directive. Here's the thing, though: You can be both directive and kind. Being directive does not give you permission to be mean-spirited in your delivery. Refining your communication style is very important as a leader, because words matter to people. The best leaders have their people's best interest at heart, and so that is where the message should be coming from to be the most effective.

In thinking about global teams, I received a great piece of advice during my interview with Cathy Susie, VP of Human Resources at Schneider Electric:

A challenge with working with people from around the world is that we are too reliant on email. It is easier for you to fire off an email than to schedule a call at 10 p.m. Don't take the easy way out just because it's more efficient.

There will be many opportunities in the near future for driving teams through challenging times. With technological advances, the speed and voracity of change are hitting everyone. How do we help our teams through this? This is where you need to be savvy in change management; it will be a necessary skill for all leaders to excel in the next 10 years and beyond. Helping your team adapt to what is coming while having a positive outlook and attitude will make a world of a difference in how you approach your work. But be careful; there is a balance between holding teams together and getting results without burning them out in the process. Burnout is the leading cause of absenteeism and health issues down the line. Be aware of this in your teams and address it as you see it pop up. Helping your team members prioritize what is important to focus on and where they should spend their time will help conquer a seemingly endless list of must-do's. It's about focusing on a few things and doing them right while building confidence within the team.

"Change is the law of life. And those who look only to the past or the present are certain to miss the future."
John F. Kennedy

Here is a great piece of insight from one of my interviews with *Michael Ratican,* a senior leader in the biotech industry at Global Training & Development at Amgen®:

Good managers recognize that there's an energy flow within their organizations, and either they're astute to it or they think their people are managing it, or not. Any manager can demand expectations or set goals—that's easy. But if you don't have the right culture and energy, then you're a mess.

Perfectionism

This leads me to another characteristic to recognize in your team—perfectionism. Believe me, I am guilty of it! But it is not your friend and will hold you back from reaching your potential. We do not have the luxury of being perfect in this fast-moving world. I have coached many people in the idea of "good enough." This is very difficult for some people, including myself. However, perfectionism does not serve us well. To hold onto this mentality will eat you alive.

That is, perfectionism can lead to burnout. In those who are perfectionist, you will see higher levels of burnout because they can't say "no," or they want everything to be the best it can be every time. Finding the balance between perfect and good enough is a skill that can be learned, but it needs to be practiced and encouraged. At the end of the day, to be perfect all the time is not worth it, and you and your team will not be recognized for this extra work. In fact, I would go as far as to say it is detrimental to your organization, because agility and speed are key to success and to being competitive in the future.

"Learning is going to be everyone's adventure. If we stop learning we stop growing, leaders especially need to be open to self-reflection, feedback and insight, without it we can't be authentic."

Michael Ratican,
Global Training & Development at Amgen

Key Takeaways:

✓ Stop firefighting and take charge by taking back control of your work life. If you spend more time looking ahead and understanding what larger business results you are trying to achieve, you can be more proactive in your career and less stressed by meaningless activity.

✓ Be purposeful with how you are spending your time. Part of your job as a leader is to develop your team. Leading requires inspiration and influence, so be sure to leverage both of these and limit your time on tasks that might seem important in the moment, but don't add any strategic value to you or your team.

✓ Focus on developing healthy habits within and outside work so you can focus with more clarity and be more productive. Our work hours have expanded, but we can use some of the downtime when waiting for information to take care of ourselves and to foster quality relationships.

✓ By demonstrating vulnerability as a leader, you show your imperfections, and research has shown that builds trust with your employees.

✓ People follow authentic leaders. You need to develop your own self-awareness and determine where you have blind spots, biases, and preferences. This will help you be a better leader, because you will recognize those times when you have a differing viewpoint that could limit your capacity for empathy.

✓ Find the human connection to those on your team and other you work with. Employees don't want to feel expendable or like just a number. This is most critical with virtual teams, because you don't have the benefit of seeing team members in the office every day.

✓ Focus your efforts as a leader on working through "learning lessons" instead of framing situations as failures. Flexibility can work in a few ways. By allowing your employees to determine *how* they will approach tasks versus the *what,* you can observe their thought processes and approaches, which can give you better insight on best ways to coach them through challenges.

Being a Visionary Leader

If you recall from earlier in the book, a visionary leader is what I describe as my Mount Fiji leadership style. In my consulting practice and my own professional career, I have seen the difficultly in using this style as an asset when it is needed. As with defining what good leadership looks like, leaders have the most difficulty in understanding what it takes to lead with a vision but simultaneously drive others to act on your vision. In this last chapter, I wanted to spend some time exploring this leadership style in more detail.

Life is interesting and life is strange. I've had my share of interesting twists and turns throughout the years of my personal and professional life. Life takes us to places we never thought or dreamed we would go. By leveraging these experiences, we can accomplish our goals and dreams to reach the summit of our potential as leaders. I say this because to drive change in any organization isn't an easy road; it takes courage. That being said, someone has to do it, and as a leader you need to do it well.

To drive your organization, you need to know what and why you are doing what you do. As humans, we are drawn to those who have the confidence to lead the path. For better or worse, it has been proven in history. So, I encourage you, as a leader in your organization, to shape the vision you would like to create—in a team, a department, or as the CEO of an organization. "How do I make sure this vision is clear to all whom I am leading?" you might be asking. It is a good question, and I hope to clarify it now with my proven techniques.

> *"If you are working on something exciting that you really care about, you don't have to be pushed. The vision pulls you."*
> Steve Jobs

I was not given a manager role officially until later in my career. Not to say that I hadn't filled leadership roles throughout my life; that hasn't been a problem. I just hadn't filled this type of role in my professional life. My first leadership role goes back to my childhood. My sister and I loved to create pseudo organizations, and we would swap being the president or secretary. It was very serious. We had dues and would collect our hard-earned allowance. We would also do fundraisers for our organization around the neighborhood. At the time, it was all fun and games, but I now realize it was training for both of us in our future careers.

Those were easier times, and we could experiment. In looking back, I now realize how important those experiences were. We were testing leadership styles, gaining donors, and testing fundraising techniques. Oh yes, as preteens we were testing the boundaries. These experiences have shaped my view on what works in leadership and how best to apply the principles I believe work today.

Topics covered in this chapter include:

- Clarity
- Diversity
- Recognition
- Exemplary leadership
- Potential and performance

"By leadership we mean the art of getting someone else to do something that you want done because he wants to do it."
Dwight D. Eisenhower

Clarity

The first step to shaping a vision is clarity. What do you or your organization want to accomplish? As a leader, you need to clearly convey the goals. Where are you steering the boat? What end goal are you aiming for? What change do you want to see in the world? These are important questions to answer if anyone will follow you in the first place. It doesn't matter if you are an owner of a company or a leader of a small team, or somewhere in between, what really matters is that the people you are leading know which direction they are going.

In current times, where change is the constant and technology is reshaping industries, the vision is critical to the success of your organization. The pace of change and technology are so vast that many in the workforce are being left behind. We cannot cling to what worked previously, but rather need to have an ever-evolving viewpoint of what will work in the future. At the same time, we as leaders need to create clarity around where we drive our organizations; otherwise, we lose energy, and complacency will replace productivity.

As leaders, we are responsible for providing focus. Workers can toil many hours and not produce anything. I am seeing that with my clients on a daily basis. There is so much wasted time and energy being put into things that do not matter. To be an effective leader, you need to provide the focus on what matters most—that is, what will accomplish the goal that is most important to your organization. Otherwise, you are leaving it to chance how your employees understand they need to spend their time. When I am working with organizations, the first thing I do is make sure I understand how they want me to spend my time. It isn't really how I do what I do that matters; it's more about determining what is important for me to do based on what the organization wants to accomplish. As Lewis Carroll once said, "If you don't know where you are going, any road will get you there." In leading your organization, you do not want to be seen as unfocused. You need to face your fears and show a strong front to whomever you are leading; otherwise they will doubt your leadership.

This is a not a path for the weak or undetermined. You will be challenged by others, and so the conviction you have as a leader is key to how successful you will be with your teams. In thinking about leveraging technology, lacking conviction is a real and constant threat to your success. How often are you gathering data on how the world is changing and evolving? You will need to understand how the external environment is impacting or will impact the direction of your organization. I suggest keeping up with trends in artificial intelligence, machine learning, block chain, and so forth, along with globalization and how it will impact where the talent lies. All of these are shaping and shifting our working environments in the very near future. Be sure you don't get left behind!

Diversity

Another key to leadership strength is the ability to create cognitive diversity in your team. What is that? It is your ability to infuse varying thoughts, perspectives and viewpoints. This starts with the moment you are hiring new people or shifting teams around. It goes beyond color, religion, sex, country, or education. What matters more is that you seek out those who clearly have a different view of the world or who bring in different perspectives. If you hire or work with people who have views similar to your own or have identical backgrounds, you are not getting diversity of thought, which is a competitive disadvantage for organizations. In fact, venture capitalists and investors decide who they will invest in by looking for diversity at all levels of organizations. There is clear research now pointing to those companies that are more diverse and encourage diversity of thought having better long-term returns for investors. One way to build diversity is to bring in new team members from cultures that are not individualistic, but more collective; or to hire someone who grew up in rural areas and not the city. Our environment and how we grew up shape our perspective of the world, and this is what I want to tap into for innovation and coming up with the best solutions moving forward.

A recent *Forbes* article on visionary leaders also pointed to expanding diversity of thoughts:

> *The most effective leaders understand they may not have all the answers and are open to those who might. They encourage new ideas from all levels and particularly appreciate the viewpoints of those closest to the problem.*[25]

For a team with diverse perspectives to work, you need to be open to varying approaches and incorporate them toward what you need to accomplish. The process of exploring differing viewpoints about possible change is called *creative tension*. You, as the leader, need to create trust for these discussions to flourish. You need to teach your team to be inclusive and critically think about what ideas should move forward and what would best serve your organization and customers. There is no place for backstabbing or gossiping, because these will kill any trust you have built. If you have any of these behaviors going on, you and your team cannot succeed in this fast-changing environment. Leaders need to represent and encourage collaboration. Your team will take the cues from you, so be sure you are acting in the way you want your team to behave.

Recognition of High Performing Team Members

If you want to foster a dream team, you need to give all the credit to them. Believe me; they will respect you more if you do so. Again, you need to realize it is not about you and your career. If you foster new leaders in the organization or get the best out of people, this will reflect on your ability to lead. If you want to snuff out all of the loyalty in your team, do the opposite of my advice and take the credit or maybe, even worse, don't recognize them at all. I have experienced both of these and can attest that they feel equally demotivating. I remember sitting in a staff meeting one time after we had worked 14–18-hour days for weeks to get this launch out in time for our customers. My manager stood there in that meeting with our senior leaders and took credit for all that we had accomplished as a team. The rest of us looked at one another in disbelief that she had the audacity to take credit for something she didn't roll her sleeves up and put work into. I couldn't believe it! Unfortunately, our senior leaders at the time were guilty of this behavior as well and did not pick up on our distress. In fact, I don't even think they cared. They were just glad the project was done on time. This is truly poor leadership in action.

One last example of lack of leadership that leads to discouragement within a team is lack of recognition of those who contributed the most. There are different schools of thought on how individuals like to be recognized, but all individuals need recognition for a job that is truly above and beyond. Otherwise, what you will be left with is average efforts. Think about it. If you and your team are willing to put in extra hours, go the extra mile to please your customers, or take on an initiative that is beyond your normal day-to-day duties, then you should be recognized appropriately as an individual or as a team.

I worked for a vice president who outright refused to recognize individual contributions on projects in front of the rest of the organization. We had a global all-staff meeting, and all the other department VPs were talking about their employees' contributions to successes in working with their top clients. A few of us looked at one another and smiled, thinking that our VP would similarly recognize our efforts in completing key client deliverables. He didn't say a word. How disappointing this opportunity was missed! Right after the meeting, one of the other senior leaders and I asked him why, when given the opportunity to highlight how our team contributed to this particular success, he chose not to. He responded that he didn't want to make anyone feel bad. Well, in passing over this opportunity, he did quite a bit of damage and caused our departments to feel devalued and unmotivated. This lack of recognition would have long-term implications for our willingness to go above and beyond for future client engagements. It was one incident, but it tarnished our future relationship and my viewpoint on his leadership, or lack thereof. Always value your team and be sure to show them how much. Recognition *does* matter to people who work for you and can be a deciding factor in causing them to leave the organization or, worse yet, stay and be demotivated and unproductive.

Exemplary Leadership

Think of some examples of visionary leaders and how they are championing their causes. I like to point to the current Dalai Lama, who is the spiritual leader of the Tibetan people. I had an opportunity to hear him speak a few years back when he was a keynote at the California Women's Conference spearheaded by Maria Shriver. I will never forget him and his powerful message of hope in the face of enormous obstacles. As you might be aware, the Chinese government took over Tibet in 1951, and he fled persecution from the government in 1959. From that time on, he has fought for the rights of the Tibetan people and is a strong advocate of uniting religions around the world. I would describe his style as a dichotomy of wisdom and childlike curiosity. He could have disappeared after he escaped from Tibet. But instead he worked tirelessly toward peaceful and thoughtful interventions of the world's ills. He has the social media reach of more than 8.6 million Twitter followers. His words are inspirational and made an impact on me.

I describe this leader because you don't need to be recognized as a leader throughout the world, but only to those you lead. You will have a huge impact if you do this right. As it is difficult to define great leadership, we can think of particular leaders that most of us know and can explore how their predominate leadership styles impact their effectiveness.

Potential and Performance

There is much talk about finding purpose in your work nowadays. The vision you create needs to tie back to your employee's purpose. If it doesn't, then you will not get the performance you would like from your team. Think about it. If you don't really believe in the mission and values of your organization, then why would you put forth much effort to help the organization meet its goals? You know those employees who show up to work and just have a job versus viewing their work as a career. Those are two different mindsets. The power in creating a vision that ties to their purpose leads to great potential and performance.

Purpose ⇔ Vision = Potential + Performance

In my interview with the CEO of WD-40 Company, Garry Ridge, he spoke of this power:

> *I look back over the time that I've been here as CEO and how we've really given people the opportunity to be part of something bigger than themselves, to learn something new every day, and to be happy. I'm proud that I got the opportunity to plant some seeds with people that people have harvested and grown. So, it's all about the people.*

He also spoke of the value of engagement in our workforce:

> *The fact is that 67% of people who go to work every day are either disengaged or actively disengaged because of the soul-sucking leadership that happens. It's because ego is eating empathy instead of empathy eating ego. There's an enormous ability to unlock productivity if we could get that number up. In 384 BC, Aristotle said, "Pleasure in the job puts perfection in the work." As leaders, we don't always create that [environment] because ego takes over and we don't practice servant leadership.*

How do we make this dream leadership style a reality? It takes time and, as Garry mentioned, dropping your ego and focusing on your team and their needs. Yes, you are setting the direction, but not how it is best to get there. Consider this analogy. You are the captain of your ship. You map out the endpoint you need or want to get to. Your crew will figure out the best path forward to get to that destination. As you are sailing on the journey, you will experience challenges, such as storms, icebergs, and even land you didn't know existed. These will cause you to have to make adjustments. These are normal and expected, because we do not know what the future really holds. The important point is that after an adjustment, the crew (like a team or an organization) is still able to see the destination on the horizon and feel confident they will get there regardless. Think of yourself as the captain of your team, guiding them in the organizational journey. Your words, actions, and mindset matter to all of them, and you need to be cognizant of that fact.

"Good leaders have vision and inspire others to help them turn vision into a reality. Great leaders have vision, share vision, and inspire others to create their own."

Roy T. Bennett,
Author of *The Light in the Heart*

You now have all the tools to be successful in adapting to the future of work and being a top of the mountain leader. In thinking about your journey to the top, test out a few of my suggestions and see how they work for you. Be sure to observe and get feedback on how you applied the strategy. You may not get it right the first time but be patient with yourself. It will get easier and, before you know it, it will become second nature. Your teams will notice the change and appreciate your efforts.

Take those steps to reach your summit to great leadership!

Key Takeaways:

✓ As a leader, you need to be clear on the "what" and "why" you are driving toward because employees are drawn to confident leaders.

✓ Don't try to boil the ocean. Focus on fewer things that have the greatest impact versus trying to do everything.

✓ It is critical to do your research on the latest in technology and what is going on in the global marketplace. Do not become complacent because you will quickly fall behind your competition. Even better, encourage your organization to constantly learn new things and give them the space to apply what they have learned.

✓ Seek diversity on your teams as much as possible. Fight the urge to build teams with those who think like you do. Research over the last 10 years has shown higher returns for those organizations that embrace variety in thought and perspectives.

✓ People want to work for leaders who recognize their efforts in achieving goals. If you don't recognize successful efforts, employee morale and productivity will take a turn for the worse.

✓ Your vision needs to tie to a larger purpose. You need to hire employees who are passionate about the same purpose; otherwise, you risk having low engagement.

✓ Leaders need to drop their egos and tap more into being empathetic. Employees have choices for where they work. Remember this when thinking about how you engage and treat your employees.

ENDNOTES

[1] Douglas Riddle, *Executive Integration: Equipping Transitioning Leaders for Success* (Greensboro, NC: Center for Creative Leadership, 2016), https://www.ccl.org/wp-content/uploads/2015/04/ExecutiveIntegration.pdf.

[2] Helen Barrett, "Plan for five careers in a lifetime," *Financial Times,* September 5, 2017, https://www.ft.com/content/0151d2fe-868a-11e7-8bb1-5ba57d47eff7.

[3] Paul Leinwand, Cesare Mainardi, and Art Kleiner, "Only 8% of Leaders Are Good at Both Strategy and Execution," *Harvard Business Review,* December 30, 2015, https://hbr.org/2015/12/only-8-of-leaders-are-good-at-both-strategy-and-execution.

[4] Douglas A. Ready, Linda A. Hill, and Robert J. Thomas, "Building a Game-Changing Talent Strategy," *Harvard Business Review* 92, nos. 1–2 (January–February 2014): 62–68.

[5] Colin Beames, *Workforce Strategy: Audit Survey Report* (London, UK: Corporate Research Forum, March, 2015), https://home.kpmg/content/dam/kpmg/pdf/2015/08/workforce-strategy-audit-survey-report.pdf.

[6] Snook, Scott, Nohria, Nitin and Khurana, Rakesh. *The Handbook for Teaching Leadership: Knowing, Doing, and Being.* (Thousand Oaks, CA. SAGE Publications, Inc. 2012)

[7] ATD Research. "Upskilling and Reskiling: Turning Disruption and Change Into New Capabillities." Quote page 4. June 2018

[8] Adkins, Amy. "Millennials: The Job-Hopping Generation." May 12, 2016

[9] Adam Bluestein, "Doctor 2.0: The Hope—And Hype—Surrounding AI Use in Healthcare," *Fast Company,* (November 2018): 32.

[10] Malcolm Frank, Paul Roehrig, and Ben Pring, *What to Do When Machines Do Everything: How to Get Ahead in a World of AI, Algorithms, Bots, and Big Data* (Hoboken, NJ: Wiley, 2017).

[11] Christopher Mims, "Inside the New Industrial Revolution," *Wall Street Journal,* November 12, 2018.

[12] *Latest report on state of U.S. science enterprise shows America leads as China rapidly advances global position in S&T* (Alexandria, VA: National Science Foundation, January 18, 2018), https://www.nsf.gov/nsb/news/news_summ.jsp?cntn_id=244252&org=NSB.

[13] Only One-Quarter of Employers Are Sustaining Gains From Change Management Initiatives (London, UK: Willis Towers Watson, August 29, 2013), https://www.towerswatson.com/en/Press/2013/08/Only-One-Quarter-of-Employers-Are-Sustaining-Gains-From-Change-Management.

[14] StrengthsFinder 2.0 [now CliftonStrengths], https://www.gallupstrengthscenter.com.

[15] *Putting Artificial Intelligence to Work,* Report From HBR Live Event Series (*Harvard Business Review,* 2018),

https://www.sas.com/content/dam/SAS/documents/event-
collateral/2018/en/putting-artificial-intelligence-to-work-series-report.pdf.

[16] Gary Hamel and Michele Zanini, "The End of Bureaucracy: How a
Chinese appliance maker is reinventing management for the digital age,"
Harvard Business Review (November–December 2018): 51.

[17] Putting Artificial Intelligence to Work, 6.

[18] Jeffrey Tjendra, "The Origins of Design Thinking," *Wired*, April, 2014,
https://www.wired.com/insights/2014/04/origins-design-thinking.

[19] Jo Szczepanska, "Design thinking origin story plus some of the people
who made it all happen," *Medium*, January 3, 2017,
https://medium.com/@szczpanks/design-thinking-where-it-came-from-and-the-
type-of-people-who-made-it-all-happen-dc3a05411e53.

[20] Stephanie Vozza, "Why Employees at Apple and Google Are More
Productive," *Fast Company*, March 13, 2017,
https://www.fastcompany.com/3068771/how-employees-at-apple-and-google-
are-more-productive.

[21] *Manager/Supervisor's Role In Change Management*, Prosci Thought
Leadership Articles, https://www.prosci.com/resources/articles/manager-change-
management-role.

[22] Scott D. Anthony, S. Patrick Viguerie, Evan I. Schwartz, and Van
Landeghem, *2018 Corporate Longevity Forecast: Creative Destruction is
Accelerating* (February 2018), https://www.innosight.com/insight/creative-
destruction.

[23] Frank, Roehrig, and Pring, *What To Do When Machines Do Everything*.

[24] Brené Brown, "The power of vulnerability," filmed June 2010 at
TEDxHouston, Houston, TX, video, 20:13,
https://www.ted.com/talks/brene_brown_on_vulnerability?language=en#t-
664000.

[25] Susan Taylor, "How to Be A Visionary Leader," *Forbes*, November 17,
2017, https://www.forbes.com/sites/forbescoachescouncil/2017/11/17/how-to-
be-a-visionary-leader/#5c3a9dd61a44.